Children, Teachers and Learning Series
General Editor: Cedric Cullingford

Children and Primary Science

Children and Primary Science

Tina Jarvis

CASSELL NICHOLS PUBLISHING

Published in Great Britain by **Cassell Educational Limited**
Villiers House, 41/47 Strand, London WC2N 5JE, England

Published in the United States of America by **Nichols Publishing**
11 Harts Lane, East Brunswick, NJ 08816, USA

First published 1991
Reprinted 1991

British Library Cataloguing in Publication Data
Jarvis, Tina
    Children and primary science. — (Children, teachers and
    learning series)
    1. Primary schools. Curriculum subjects: Science, teaching
    I. Title   II. Series

ISBN 0-304-32264-4 (Cassell hardback)
        0-304-32270-9 (Cassell paperback)
        0-89397-413-7 (Nichols paperback)

Typeset by Colset Pte. Ltd, Singapore
Printed and bound in Great Britain by
Biddles Ltd, Guildford and King's Lynn

Contents

Many thanks to my husband Peter and to Frieda Billingham for their valuable advice and support

Foreword

The books in this series stem from the conviction that all those who are concerned with education should have a deep interest in the nature of children's learning. Teaching and policy decisions ultimately depend on an understanding of individual personalities accumulated through experience, observation and research. Too often in recent years decisions on the management of education have had little to do with the realities of children's lives, and too often the interest shown in the performance of teachers, or in the content of the curriculum, has not been balanced by an interest in how children respond to either. The books in this series are based on the conviction that children are not fundamentally different from adults, and that we understand ourselves better by our insight into the nature of children.

The books are designed to appeal to *all* those who are interested in education and who take it as axiomatic that anyone concerned with human nature, culture or the future of civilization is interested in education – in the individual process of learning, as well as what can be done to help it. While each book draws on recent findings in research and is aware of the latest developments in policy, each is written in a style that is clear, readable and free from the jargon that has undermined much scholarly writing, especially in such a relatively new field of study.

Although the audience to be addressed includes all those concerned with education, the most important section of the audience is made up of professional teachers, the teachers who continue to learn and grow and who need both support and stimulation. Teachers are very busy people, whose energies are taken up in coping with difficult circumstances. They deserve material that is stimulating, useful and free of jargon and is in tune with the practical realities of classrooms.

Each book is based on the principle that the study of education is a discipline in its own right. There was a time when the study of the principles of learning and the individual's response to his or her environment was a collection of parts of other disciplines – history, philosophy, linguistics, sociology and psychology. That time is assumed to be over and the books address those who are interested in the study of children and how they respond to their environment.

Each book is written both to enlighten the readers and to offer practical help to develop their understanding. They therefore not only contain accounts of what we understand about children, but also illuminate these accounts by a series of examples, based on observation of practice. These examples are designed not as a series of rigid steps to be followed, but to show the realities on which the insights are based.

Most people, even educational researchers, agree that research on children's learning has been most disappointing, even when it has not been completely missing. Apart from the general lack of a 'scholarly' educational tradition, the inadequacies of such study come about because of the fear of approaching such a complex area as children's inner lives. Instead of answering curiosity with observation, much educational research has attempted to reduce the problem to simplistic solutions, by isolating a particular hypothesis and trying to improve it, or by trying to focus on what is easy and 'empirical'. These books try to clarify the real complexities of the problem, and are willing to be speculative.

The real disappointment with educational research, however, is that it is very rarely read or used. The people most at home with children are often unaware that helpful insights can be offered to them. The study of children and the understanding that comes from self-knowledge are too important to be left to obscurity. In the broad sense real 'research' is carried out by all those engaged in the task of teaching or bringing up children.

All the books share a conviction that the inner worlds of children repay close attention, and that much subsequent behaviour and attitudes depend upon the early years. They also share the conviction that children's natures are not markedly different from those of adults, even if they are more honest about themselves. The process of learning is reviewed as the individual's close and idiosyncratic involvement in events, rather than the passive reception of, and processing of, information.

Cedric Cullingford

Preface

Since the introduction of the National Curriculum, science has been given a new and exciting emphasis in the primary classroom. As one of the three core subjects it now has the same importance as English and mathematics. English and mathematics are essentially languages which enable us to communicate about the world we find ourselves in, and science assists understanding of that world.

Good science teaching encourages children to think imaginatively, creatively and logically. In this rapidly changing world children need such abilities in order to respond to technological advances and to understand their implications. Science teaching also helps children to understand and respect their environment so that they can appreciate the need to promote care for conservation of the world's resources.

Teachers are already doing a lot of science but perhaps have not identified it as such. Studies of human biology, plants, animals and the natural and the man-made environments are already incorporated in many classroom activities. The teacher can build on this knowledge to incorporate investigatory skills and add the aspects of physical science required by the National Curriculum. This book therefore intends to concentrate on those science topics, such as forces, materials and energy, that are least familiar to teachers and to demonstrate how practical investigative skills can be incorporated into biological activities.

Although there is an extensive amount of knowledge to be covered in the National Curriculum, scientific skills are equally important. It is important not to overlook the fact that, when children are assessed, Attainment Target 1, which incorporates the skill element, has a weighting of 50 per cent in key stage 1 and 45 per cent in key stage 2. Consequently the development of these skills should be an integral part of all activities. The National Curriculum makes it clear that children should develop these scientific skills through very practical, first-hand experiences which involve children in their own observations, explorations and investigations. Children thrive on practical science activities. They become highly motivated, which usually has a positive effect on related areas of the curriculum, as follow-up written, mathematical and art work is enhanced. The first chapter of this book considers how practical investigatory science can be developed.

Becoming aware of the properties, potentials and limitations of materials is fundamental to many practical primary activities. Children's art, craft and technology in particular will be enhanced by this knowledge. Investigatory science both helps to provide this knowledge and benefits from studying materials. Consequently, the second chapter considers how materials might be explored and investigated throughout the primary school.

Subsequent chapters concentrate on activities that help children at key stage 1 to develop observational and early investigation skills through studying the environment, and by using play equipment that encourages an early understanding of forces and energy.

This section is followed by those topics, such as magnetism, electricity and light, that span the later years of key stage 1 and early years of key stage 2. Finally, the last section includes topics for children working at key stage 2. It is not possible to cover activities that are based on using secondary sources. Nor can the book hope to suggest in detail extension activities for the very able 10-year-old.

Hopefully this book will reassure, encourage and help teachers to try more practical investigatory science in order to discover for themselves how exciting and stimulating science can be for pupils and teachers alike.

An International View

Educationalists all over the world have recognized that a new approach to teaching science is needed, as is illustrated by recent reports emanating from a number of sources worldwide. Consequently the strategies described in this book are not relevant purely to the United Kingdom, but have wider significance. They will have particular value for schools in North America, where developments in science teaching are very similar.

In the United States of America recent studies have shown that there is a need to provide additional support to teachers engaged in teaching science to young children. J. Goodlad, for example, in his 1984 book *A Place Called School: Prospects for the Future* (New York: McGraw-Hill) reports on one of the most extensive classroom investigations yet carried out in the United States. It involved in-depth investigations of 1016 classrooms and questioned 1350 teachers. He points out that elementary school teachers stated that they wanted students to be able to compare and contrast phenomena, explore the interrelationships among living things, interpret environmental changes, make inferences from data, formulate hypotheses, observe and classify, and develop skills of inquiry. However, Goodlad's observations in the classroom indicated that the gap between these expectations and actual teaching practices was considerable.

The existence of such a gap suggests that many American teachers do not have the expertise at present to teach higher levels of science thinking because their own education did not include these skills. In the same way British teachers are on the whole keen to respond to the needs of their Science National Curriculum, which encourages these very skills, but they currently lack the expertise and confidence. Thus it is likely that the attempts in the United Kingdom to implement the National Curriculum in Science will be of special interest to American educators.

This book aims to help teachers implement the National Curriculum's proposals by moving away from a purely factual approach to develop a more varied science programme based on developing the children's scientific thinking and concepts. It also attempts to explain the phenomena and results from experiments that the children should discover in order both to inform and give confidence to the teachers.

American schools, like their English counterparts, teach common topics in the first three grades which include animals, plants, seasons, heat, light, colour, sound, magnets and machines. These are further developed in the upper elementary grades along with the solar system, weather and climate, simple ecological systems and electricity. Consequently there is much in this book that the North American teacher, in particular, will feel is both relevant and basically familiar.

It is hoped that the book will help elementary teachers in many other countries and particularly those in the United States, as well as British teachers, to build on their knowledge and expertise to provide a more practical and investigatory style of science in their classrooms which will benefit all pupils.

CHAPTER 1
Teaching Primary Science

Approaching the teaching of science

An emphasis on first-hand practical activities is essential. These can include teacher-initiated activities intended to focus the children's attention on particular concepts; opportunities for play and free exploration of provided materials; and open-ended problem-solving activities. Alongside these practical activities the children need plenty of opportunities to work in small groups and talk about their investigations and discoveries.

Work based on first-hand experiences makes science stimulating and relevant, and enables a wide range of skills to be developed. Observing and using real things enables the children to use all their senses. They can appreciate comparative sizes, textures, distances, smells, etc. When they carry out simple experiments for themselves the experience is more lasting and the concepts involved clearer than when secondary sources are used. It is also easier for the teacher to recognize when a concept is misunderstood or if language is used inappropriately.

Throughout the primary school children need opportunities to 'play' with new materials and equipment. For example, when children are given mirrors for the first time they need a time to explore them. They will then be able to participate more effectively in discussion by suggesting properties they have already discovered. They are also more likely to concentrate on a specific investigation when the initial novelty has worn off slightly. Often children also need a chance for a free time of exploration after a set activity. When children have completed an investigation provided by the teacher, if they can continue to use the materials in a 'play' or undirected time they are able to consolidate the concepts involved and to try out their own ideas that were prompted by the task.

Whenever possible, science activities should include an open-ended element. If the children are given a 'recipe' for an activity or investigation, their ingenuity and imagination will not be developed. They are more likely to learn how to set up a 'fair' experiment, raise their own questions, suggest hypotheses and interpret data if they are involved in the decision-making process. The children could discuss and plan the investigation with the teacher before starting. On another occasion the teacher may provide the basic instructions but expect the children to make decisions during the investigation for themselves. The children can also be encouraged to raise their own questions during the work, which are then investigated later on their own. For example, the children might be asked how they could set about testing whether the depth of soil is important for successful survival of seeds, rather than simply being told what to do. Once a method has been decided the children can be encouraged to agree among themselves how to measure and record the differences in growth. After completing the experiment the children may suggest other factors of growth which they can investigate, following the procedure that they have just used.

If the work is both practically based and has an open-ended problem-solving element, all children can participate effectively at their own particular intellectual level. The less able children understand what is happening because it is tangible and immediate. They will often arrive at a solution, although one probably not as sophisticated as their peers; and they are less restricted by the requirement to read before being able to join in effectively. The very able child, on the other hand, is able to investigate and solve problems in a more advanced way.

Young children will have already developed a set of beliefs to handle everyday events. They assume a kettle will boil when heated; predict where to catch a thrown ball; and say the sun moves across the sky. These beliefs are founded on many experiences and are often related to the way words are interpreted in common use. The term 'light', for example, is used in everyday conversations in a different way than when used by a physicist. Consequently the children's ideas may not always accord with those that the teacher wishes to develop. When new experiences are provided the children will not necessarily modify their views immediately, despite evidence to the contrary. At times they may even appear to hold conflicting ideas simultaneously. This is quite normal. Plenty of practical opportunities are needed to enable them to accept alternative interpretations as well as to confirm accepted beliefs. These can be provided during structured investigations initiated by the teacher, as part of testing their own hypotheses and during 'play' or undirected time.

The children need opportunities to make their ideas explicit and to raise their own scientific questions by talking to the teacher and to other children in an atmosphere that welcomes and treats their ideas with respect. This enables the teacher to judge the development of the children's concepts and the children to listen to and evaluate other ideas. Initially the teacher may have to ask questions and suggest problems and different explanations to demonstrate that this is acceptable behaviour. If there is plenty of guided open-ended experimental work and discussion in the early years the children, as they get older, will be more confident in suggesting explanations and better prepared to suggest their own ideas for investigations and ways to carry them out.

Oral and listening skills are not only required by the National Curriculum for both English and science, but discussion also enhances scientific understanding. When the children talk about their work to the teacher or to their peers their skills of description, questioning, analysis and negotiation are improved. The children are also helped to clarify their ideas and subsequent written work is invariably enhanced.

Practical and oral work means that the children need to work in groups. If the children work in pairs or small groups they are able to share ideas and participate fully. In large groups there is a tendency for some children not to be fully involved. Group work also enables the less able to be supported and assisted by the others, helping to improve their self-image as they become effective members of a team.

Ideally everyday materials, tools and basic measuring equipment required to make models and carry out tests should be easily visible and available to the children. When the children are given an open-ended problem, if they can see what is available it stimulates their imagination and prompts improvisation.

Most experiments or investigations for primary school children are very simple and require a limited range of equipment at any one time. This has the advantage that once the children have had experience of carrying out investigations under the direction of the teacher, they should increasingly be able to suggest, plan and set up investigations for themselves.

When organizing the timetable it is important to remember that practical science takes time. The children need plenty of opportunity to discuss the problem; set up and carry out the activity; and record or report their findings. This may take a whole morning or in some cases a day. This may seem to require a high percentage of the time available, but many science activities support other areas of the curriculum. Mathematics is used in a real and relevant context, motivating children to use their mathematical skills in an accurate way. Many English, geography, technology and art skills can be incorporated within science work.

Increasing teacher confidence

Initially teachers may themselves feel apprehensive about providing open-ended practical activities. Some are concerned that discipline might be difficult to maintain or that they will be unable to answer the children's questions. Children are very keen to join in the practical activities and usually become too involved to be naughty. The teacher can make it clear to the children that if they are disruptive they will only be allowed to watch. The children may be excited during the first practical activities, so the teacher must distinguish between misbehaviour and fairly noisy enthusiastic interest which is on task.

Although teachers may need to extend their knowledge in some areas, particularly in aspects relating to forces and energy, they do not need a great depth of scientific knowledge. They do need to be open-minded, however, and to allow children to be curious and to think about what they experience and to question it. When the teachers occasionally state that they do not know an answer the children have an excellent role model to follow. In a supportive atmosphere children will feel confident to admit if they do not know or understand something. Some of the questions raised by children may be answerable by investigations or by recourse to books. However, there are some questions that are too complex, are inappropriate or cannot be tackled because of limited time or resources. Children need to feel that they can investigate their own ideas, but it is not necessary to investigate every question raised to provide a balanced scientific programme.

A lot of expensive material is not necessary to enable the children to pursue a broad, balanced and practical science programme. Virtually the whole of Levels 1 to 5 can be successfully covered using items found in the home and school with the addition of items such as magnets, prisms, batteries, bulbs, bells, biological collecting equipment and observing equipment, and mathematical equipment which should already be available in the school for practical mathematics. Parents may be able to help to collect equipment including junk materials, fabrics, working toys and simple household machines.

All teachers are advised to try out the investigations before presenting them to the children so that they have some idea of what problems might arise. When setting an open-ended problem for the children to solve (e.g. make something that shows how strong the wind is, make a boat that will travel across a water tank), the teacher could think of one or two solutions in advance in the unlikely event the children cannot think of anything. This is really to help the teacher feel confident, as a group of children can usually produce far more ideas than one teacher. Once an investigatory approach is tried the enthusiasm of the children and the motivation, personal and academic progress the pupils make should reassure the teacher. Teacher confidence should grow with every session.

The important message is try it! Science is exciting for teacher and pupils alike.

Developing scientific skills

There are several major scientific skills: observation, measuring and recording, investigating, prediction and hypothesizing, and communicating. There is no simple division of skills between key stages 1 and 2. Some children in the early years will be ready to develop advanced skills whereas others in junior classes will still be at a very basic stage. Teachers of the early years must be aware of what will be required later so that they can start to introduce the skills. Junior teachers need to know what has already been covered so that work can extend the children, not just repeat the basic skills.

Young children should be using all their senses to observe, sort, group and describe at first hand things in their immediate environment. These observation skills can be increasingly developed by encouraging the children to notice detailed similarities and differences; to use lenses and microscopes appropriately to improve their sense of sight; and when older to choose what is relevant to a particular problem and what is not.

The children's observations can be systematically recorded in written reports, poetry, descriptive writing, models, collage, clay, paintings, tapes, or in mathematical forms such as block graphs and bar charts.

The teacher in the early years needs to start to show the children how to carry out a 'fair' investigation. This should not be left to the junior years as the children need time to build up their expertise in order to design and carry out their own experiments. Children understand the concept of 'fair', for example, quickly pointing out if someone has one more sweet than them! However, very young children find it difficult to make sure only one variable is changed. By choosing problems that have meaning for the children, the teacher can help them to identify a few of the variables. For example, if the children are asked to find the best place to dry a teddy bear's scarves, they can be helped to see that the location is the only factor that can change in their investigation. They can place his scarves on a line, on a radiator, on a desk and in a cupboard. All other variables must be the same. The children should be able to see it is not fair to soak one scarf but put a small amount of water on the others; or to leave one to dry screwed up but the others opened flat.

As the children get older they should increasingly realize that measurements are often necessary to ensure the experiment is fair and to find the difference between results. Whenever possible the children should make decisions for themselves about what, when and how to measure. It is important, therefore, that the type of equipment and accuracy demanded for each activity reflects their mathematical development. As science enables mathematics to be used in real situations children will usually try hard to be accurate.

Prediction and hypothesis (explanation) are essential aspects of scientific method. Children find it easier to understand what prediction means. Opportunities for children to guess or predict what will happen occur in both mathematics and science. As children are very keen to be right and to please the teacher they will not take the risk of being wrong unless they are assured that it does not matter if the prediction proves to be incorrect. Initially the children tend to make wild guesses, but these improve as the children learn to look at the pattern of their observations.

Children will need considerable guidance before they can make and test hypotheses confidently. When the children have carried out a test the teacher can encourage them to make a statement or generalization about what they have observed. For example, they may be testing different materials to see if they are waterproof. After being encouraged to observe their results carefully they may say 'All red materials are waterproof'. This is an acceptable statement if it accords with what has happened in their particular experiment. They then collect a set of red materials, which they have predicted will all be waterproof. They then test again to see if they were correct. If not, they make a new statement. It does not matter if this is wrong. All tests give information. After the second test the children will be able to say 'Colour does not make any difference to whether the fabric is waterproof or not'. Such statements can be developed into truly scientific hypotheses, which explain why something happens by suggesting a cause for an observed effect. For example, the children might have seen some plants dying on a window-sill. The teacher can encourage the children to suggest why or how this has happened. Several explanations may be given: they have not been watered enough and plants need water for growth; the soil is poor and plants need minerals for life; or they have been attacked by pests which have eaten them. To test their first idea the children could water one set of plants and compare them with others that are given no water. The children need also to be helped to realize that tests should often be repeated to be sure that the observations are consistent and the first results were not a result of chance.

Ideally, by the end of key stage 2 the children should be planning and carrying out investigations for themselves. As the children gain in experience and confidence in investigations, the teacher need only set the problem and ask groups to plan and carry out the investigation independently. Once both the teacher and the children feel confident with provided investigations, the children could be encouraged to think of their own problems and carry them out fairly.

These skills should be applied and practised in a variety of contexts covering the knowledge content required by the National Curriculum. As the children learn new concepts they can also be encouraged to apply what they have learnt or recognize where it is used. Many technology activities can involve applying scientific knowledge or skills. For example, a task to design and make clothes for a teddy bear to wear in the rain might include the children applying their knowledge about materials that are waterproof.

Investigatory skills should be the foundation of all science work. Activities should aim to develop both skills and concepts in parallel.

FURTHER READING

Department of Education and Science and the Welsh Office (1989) *Science in the National Curriculum*. London: HMSO.

Driver, R., Guesne, E. and Tiberbhien, A. (eds) (1985) *Children's Ideas in Science*. Milton Keynes: Open University Press.

Harlen, W. and Jelly, S. (1989) *Developing Science in the Primary Classroom*. London: Oliver and Boyd.

Hodgson, B. and Scanlon, E. (eds) (1985) *Approaching Primary Science*. London: Harper and Row.

National Curriculum Council (1989) *Science: Non-Statutory Guidance*. York: National Curriculum Council.

Raper, G. and Stringer, J. (1987) *Encouraging Primary Science*. London: Cassell.

Exploring Materials

In the infant and early junior years emphasis is given to the exploration and investigation of the properties of materials. Since the children are expected to apply this knowledge in more complex situations in later junior years, a good foundation based on practical experience is essential.

Developing play into investigation

Initially, reception children will explore materials through play. As the children handle and play with materials they can be encouraged to notice shape, colour and texture and how materials behave when squashed, stretched, bent and twisted. A good variety of suitable materials is obviously essential so that the teacher can prompt the children to compare and contrast the properties of a wide range of substances. Consideration of the suitability of a material for a particular job helps to focus the children's attention on the properties of the material. Even reception children are able to choose a suitable material from a given range and give their reasons, e.g. the best paper for making a puppet, or the best glue for making a collage. However, they can only do this when a variety of materials is available for them to choose from. Sometimes they will choose materials which are not suitable for a particular task. However, if these 'mistakes' are treated as interesting discoveries in a supportive atmosphere the children will gain in both scientific skills and independence.

The children's exploration of materials during play can be gradually extended into more formal investigations. This development can be simplified into five general stages: undirected play, collecting and preparing material, sorting for specific properties, teacher-led simple investigations and open-ended investigations. The children will need opportunities for undirected play, directed discovery and to apply their knowledge for each type of material.

Consequently, at any one time children could be investigating different materials in all these ways.

UNDIRECTED PLAY

A carefully controlled, rich environment needs to be provided with access to a wide range of materials. This provision needs to be relatively consistent so that the children become familiar and secure in the environment and are able to change and develop their responses to the provision as they discover the potential of the materials available. The materials might include:

- junk materials; different sizes, colours and types of paper, cloth, wool or straws; sponges; stones; shells; and bits of metal for collage and modelling;
- different sizes and types of brushes;
- dry and wet sand to show different conditions for pouring or moulding; clay and dough for twisting, moulding and modelling;
- water, funnels, tubes, containers and bottles of different sizes;
- clothes (for role play and drama) of different colours, textures, materials, weights and sizes;
- natural and treated wood varying in thickness, roughness and size;
- construction materials of various sizes, colours, shapes and materials.

As the children play with, use and explore the characteristics and potential of the equipment and materials the teacher intervenes at appropriate moments to talk, question or extend each child's activity. As it can take considerable time for all the materials to be explored fully, records of each child's activity and how he or she interacts with the materials are needed so that the teacher knows when and how to intervene. The teacher's careful observations, skill in knowing when to intervene at significant moments and record-keeping are the keys to developing the child's potential. Initially the very young child might ignore the material completely or have a very brief interaction with it. As the children become more aware of the potential of the material they often repeat one action. For example, they might keep dropping a stone into water.

They are testing the consistency of a characteristic or action. Often children do not want adult interference at this stage. Later they want to verbalize their observations. At this point teacher intervention is valuable to encourage the children to develop their observations by predicting what will happen after an action, i.e. the stone will drop, splash and sink; and to help the child to apply the experience to other materials.

COLLECTING AND PREPARING MATERIALS WITH THE TEACHER

As the children start to appreciate the properties of different materials the teacher can direct the children's attention to various properties or types of materials. This can be part of most of the activities in a normal infant classroom. The children helping the teacher to prepare for art or craft could be involved in cutting and sorting materials into different textures, colours and sizes. Preparing for or cleaning up after painting, washing toys or clothes enables the teacher to prompt the children to notice how different materials hold water, which materials are waterproof, which dry quickly and which places are good for drying. When the children are taken out to buy ingredients for cooking or to collect interesting items to use in the classroom they can talk about and compare the various things. Cooking enables the children to watch the changing constituency of mixtures as they are mixed or heated. Such on-going activities enable the teacher to encourage the children to observe carefully, using all their senses; to start to sort and classify in order to make meaning of their environment; and to arouse their curiosity and encourage them to question what they see.

TEACHER-LED ACTIVITIES TO SORT MATERIALS FOR A SPECIFIC PROPERTY

From a very wide provision the child's attention is drawn to one or two specific properties by the teacher. The work can be extended over time to compare different characteristics and materials.

When children are trying to explain their observations they need descriptive terms such as rough, soft, smooth or hard. This is rarely a problem for fluent English speakers but frequently causes a problem for children whose first language is not English. Practical science is a very effective medium for developing language. By 'setting' for a property only one term needs to be introduced at a time, e.g. hard and not hard. The children learn the meanings of the words more rapidly when they hear and use them in a meaningful context. Pictures are not adequate to make clear descriptive words such as rough, damp and sour.

There is considerable overlap with the development of mathematical skills as more complex setting tasks are provided. Development is shown by the child being able to:

(a) set with reference to one characteristic only: red – not red, squashy – not squashy;
(b) set with reference to two descriptors: hard – soft, wood – metal;
(c) collect additional appropriate items, other than those provided, to be included in a set;
(d) set with reference to three properties;
(e) set items which have overlapping sets: things that float – things that sink – things that float and sink; and
(f) suggest a suitable property to set items and carry out the task correctly.

Alongside this development the child can be encouraged to describe familiar objects using an increasing number of properties and using all the senses. As increased sophistication occurs, the child can be presented with unfamiliar objects and be helped to describe them using several simple properties.

TEACHER-LED SIMPLE EXPERIMENTS TO INVESTIGATE A PROPERTY

By following up the children's interests generated during play the teacher is able to extend their observation. For example, while playing with dough, two children may stretch the dough as high as they can and watch to see whose dough collapses first. The teacher might develop this interest and make different constituencies of dough with the children to see if this makes a difference. Dough which has been kept for a few days could also be used for comparison. While playing with washing clothes, the children might notice that some materials dry more quickly than others. They can then cut two or three different materials to the same size, soak them, and leave them to dry to see which dries first.

Craft and modelling should continue throughout, using as wide a variety of materials as possible with the children involved in making decisions and tests about which materials to use. Fiction and non-fiction books give frequent starting points. A story about a monster party might lead to making monster puppets, which involves trying out different glues, staples or tapes to fix a variety of cloths, paper and card. As part of the party the children might make jelly. As well as the opportunity this gives to observe how water boils, how jelly dissolves, and how the mixture sets and acts when squeezed or shaken, the children can test the effect of different amounts of water to make the jelly.

OPEN-ENDED INVESTIGATIONS OF THE PROPERTIES OF MATERIALS

Increasingly more open-ended problems requiring the use of the materials the child has been exploring can be suggested, e.g. making a boat out of paper that will float; finding the best material for a tea cosy; making a moving swing that will carry the weight of a doll; finding the most appropriate paper to cover the tables during a craft session. The children also need plenty of opportunity and encouragement to raise their own questions and investigate them.

Investigating a wide range of materials

In this way the children should be able to investigate a wide range of materials, initially in a general way and then with increasing attention to specific properties. They need opportunities to explore and investigate materials in all three states of matter in order to provide an essential foundation to enable them to classify materials into solids, liquids and gases at a later date. The remainder of the chapter will consider how young children can investigate air and other gases, liquids and a range of solid materials.

Air

WHAT IS AIR?

Activities might be initiated by the children noticing bubbles while playing with sponges or bottles in water; seeing paper blown along;

or having balloons at a party. Several activities can then be provided to extend the children's appreciation that air has substance even although it cannot be seen. Time to 'play' with similar equipment after relatively directed activities should enable the children to consolidate their understanding.

The children could be given two balloons, one inflated and one deflated, and asked to talk about each and to try to explain the differences. The children can be encouraged to experiment further with the balloons. They might be asked to blow them up and let the air come out. Can they let the air out slowly or quickly? How? Can they make different noises with the balloon? Can they suggest what is in the balloon? Even a simple question like this can lead to unexpected answers, e.g. 'God is in there!', which needs to be given as full a response as the expected reply. Other simple problems can be set. Can they stop air coming out of the balloon? What different ways can they find for getting air out of a closed balloon? Using a pin, sitting on it, pushing it or squeezing it might be suggested. Children can be shown the air is strong when it is trapped. They can try to flatten an inflated balloon without bursting it or rest a heavy brick on a tray held up by four balloons to demonstrate how tyres hold up a car. After exploring the balloons the children should be able to explain how inflatable toys, beach balls and swimming arm-bands are prepared for use and what will happen if they are mistreated and are punctured.

BUBBLES OF AIR

Opportunities to find out what happens to bubbles of air under water can be given by providing balloons, cans, straws, bottles, jars with and without lids, jugs and pumps as part of water play. Questioning helps to develop the children's observations and encourages them to become curious about what they see. The teacher might ask: which way do the bubbles move; can the children suggest why the bubbles rise; is it possible to trap air under the water?

Children enjoy blowing large soap bubbles. Again the children should observe carefully what the bubble looks like, how it moves and what happens to it. What is inside the bubble? What is trapping the air? Very creative oral and written work can develop.

The children can investigate different ways of making bubbles. They can try using their hands, wire circles, wire squares, wire spirals and so on to discover which are most effective and perhaps to suggest why. Different types of soap mixtures and strengths are other areas of investigation.

Bubble pictures can be made by blowing into water mixed with paint and a little washing up liquid. A piece of paper placed on the surface of the bubbles prints the pattern of bubbles. How can the children vary the size or number of the bubbles in the pictures?

MOVING AIR

The movement of air causes effects that demonstrate it is a real substance and that it has force. The children may be able to relate the sound of a high wind to how the air makes a sound as it escapes from a balloon. They could go on a hunt to find signs of the wind's movement and compile pictures of the wind's activity. Children who have lived in other countries may be able to share experiences of monsoon or hurricane winds.

These initial observations can be extended by asking the children to think of ways of moving a piece of paper. They might try blowing, waving something, using a balloon or by closing a door or book suddenly. A paper-blowing race could prompt tests on choosing the best paper and design for speed. They could then set up an investigation to find out which type of paper blows along quickest. To ensure that the test is 'fair' they need to use the same size paper and blow it along in the same way. Only the type of paper, such as typing, sugar or corrugated, should change. The children could also carry out a test to find the fastest flat shape. Finally they could test to find the best way of using a newspaper as a 'flapper', either rolled up or open.

It is more difficult for the wind to move heavy things. Children could test this by finding out how far they can blow a matchbox loaded with different numbers of marbles. Tests on different surfaces could also be tried. The children should try to make their tests fair and suggest reasons for their results.

HOW DOES AIR HELP US?

Whenever possible, the children should look for applications or situations that involve principles they have been learning about.

In the case of studies about air they might make pictures, models, books or collections showing how air is used. Collections could include driers, fans, bicycle pumps, blower heaters, balloons and inflatable arm-bands.

Air can be used to inflate things, often to make them float; to move things; to dry clothes; to cool people or places and to heat rooms. Using air to inflate things has already been mentioned. The idea that air can be used to move things can be extended by making kites, windmills, aeroplanes, streamers and hot-air balloons (see Chapter 4). To see how air can have a cooling effect the children could make paper fans. Simple investigations on discovering the best place to dry clothes are discussed later in this chapter.

Other gases

Most other gases are too dangerous to allow children to experiment with them. However, there may be opportunities to point out to children where other gases are used. They might have a gas oven or fire at home. They might see hot-air balloons or be given a helium balloon at a party or fair. As a general rule science for young children should be based on first-hand practical experiences. Secondary sources are only appropriate to extend practical work; to prompt ideas for practical activities; or as in this case where the children cannot handle the material for reasons of safety.

Liquids

WHAT IS A LIQUID?

There is more scope to investigate different liquids than gases.

An exploration of liquids could start with a 'liquid morning'. The children will probably have many suggestions. Preparing and clearing up food usually involves a variety of liquids. Different groups could prepare soup, jelly, runny honey sandwiches and fruit juice. Others could be painting or experimenting with water toys.

There are many cheap, safe liquids that the children can handle, e.g. water, cooking oil, honey, tomato sauce, vinegar. However, it is important to discuss the dangers of tasting or drinking unknown things before experiments. Initially the children could try to describe the liquid's colour, texture, thickness, stickiness, smell, taste and ease of pouring. Pairs of liquids can be compared to find as many characteristics that are the same or different. If the children work in pairs or small groups the quality of the observations will be improved as they stimulate each other with different ideas. From these activities the children can try to decide what the characteristics of a liquid are. They will probably suggest ideas such as 'They pour, spill and feel smooth'. This statement can be checked by collecting some different liquids and non-liquids.

It is mainly liquids that pour but some solids also appear to pour e.g. dry sand. If the children use a microscope or magnifying glass they should discover that sand is made up of many separate solid grains. A grain on its own does not pour. Dry sand can be piled up but liquids find the lowest level. The comparison of granules and liquids can be investigated further. The children could investigate ground rice, salt, rice and sugar as well as sand. They could compare how rice pours with how water pours. Do they look the same on top? What happens when the jar is tapped? What happens when the jar is tipped to one side? Hopefully the children will notice that liquids have a level surface and that liquids return to this level surface quickly after being disturbed. Liquids also fill the lowest spaces first. When water is poured into an aquarium with large stones at the bottom, the water fills all the spaces but rice has to be deliberately spread. Once the children have compared rice and water they can predict and then compare the action of another pair, e.g. milk and salt.

Water

USING WATER

A walk around the school and surrounding area will enable the children to start thinking about where and why water is used, e.g. to water plants; water for animals and people to drink; to cook food; to clean things and ourselves; and to swim in. The importance of water for living things is covered in Chapter 3.

The effectiveness of water for cleaning can be simply investigated. Four children in a group each paint their hands and let them dry. They then wash their hands to see who gets them cleanest. One child uses cold water; one cold water and soap; a third uses warm water; and the last uses warm water and soap. There are a limited number of variables so it is worth asking the children how they can make their experiment 'fair'. The amount and type of paint should be the same. The amount of water and number of hand movements during washing should also be the same. The importance of washing hands correctly for hygienic reasons is more likely to be accepted after such an activity. The same type of activity can be done with dirty cups or fabric.

WATER CAN BE CHANGED BY HEATING OR COOLING IT

Water is fascinating for children because they can see the change from a solid to a liquid to a gas. If the children watch water being boiled in a kettle with a whistle or in a saucepan with a lid, they should observe and hear the bubbles and see the steam rise. They may be able to suggest what is making the whistle or the lid rise. If a cold plate is put in the path of the steam they should see the water condense into a liquid again.

Unlike boiling water, young children can handle and experiment with ice. Making ice lollies is an exciting start to an investigation. The teacher may need to prompt the children to notice that the frozen ice lolly takes up more space than the original water. This can be followed by an investigation to find out where ice can be made. Containers of water can be placed in a variety of places, e.g. in the sun, main fridge area, freezer, dark cupboard. The children need to realize it needs to be very cold for ice to form. Top infants and older children could also leave a thermometer with the water to find out how cold it needs to be. Once the children have discovered where ice forms they could then fill containers of different sizes to see whether the amount of water makes any difference to how quickly the water freezes.

Once ice cubes have been made the children can study the rate of melting. How long do they take to melt? Where do ice cubes melt quickly or slowly. If several ice cubes of the same size are put in the same location do they melt at the same or different rates? Can the children think of a way stopping the ice cube melting? If they had an ice lolly how could they stop it melting while they took it home? If the children think of wrapping the lolly up, they could test their idea by using two ice cubes, wrapping up one and leaving the other unwrapped, and then checking what had happened after half an hour.

Children can also see how solids become liquid and vice versa when they use candles, wax in wax-resist pictures and chocolate.

WATER CAN BE CHANGED BY ADDING THINGS

Water is not always used in its pure state. It is often mixed with something else. The children will be able to think of occasions when it is mixed, e.g. with soap for cleaning; with paints to make them usable or thinner; and with colouring and other foods to make a variety of foods.

To investigate what happens when different things are mixed in water the children need a variety of soluble and insoluble things. They should mix them with water and watch carefully what happens. Things like soap powder, sugar, coffee, chalk, crayon, pencil shavings, seeds, cooking oil, soil and tomato sauce make a good start, but the children may be able to suggest other items as well. If they add the items to the water slowly they should observe not only that some things do not mix with water but also how heavy things fall to the bottom; the patterns made by other liquids as they spread through the water; that some things need to be stirred before dissolving but other do not: that the rate of dissolving varies; that some things appear to dissolve but then settle out; that some things which do not dissolve sink to the bottom while others float at the top. Only when they have had plenty of time to observe and talk about their findings should terms like 'dissolve' be introduced. They then have had practical experience to appreciate the concept.

FLOATING AND SINKING

Things that do not dissolve, float, sink or are held in suspension. Without the opportunity to experiment in water children have many misconceptions about flotation. Even 11-year-olds can say that all heavy things sink or come up with the idea that all hard, metal or glass things will sink. Without practical experience they will tend not to think of shape as a major factor.

Many teachers are concerned that a lot of experiments with water will cause an excessive amount of mess in the classroom. Covering the tables with plastic sheeting and newspaper will deal with splashes and accidental spillages. If equipment is limited, one group can do practical work while the others carry on with other work. It is also possible to work as a class by providing a washing-up bowl for every four to six children. The rule that children who are deliberately silly with the water cannot participate is a very effective sanction and if groups are expected to report about their investigations to the whole class they are motivated to participate fully. Children love experimenting with water. They become very involved in the challenges set and are normally too interested even to think about misbehaving.

Reception children need plenty of opportunity to handle a wide variety of materials in water. Different objects can be put out as part of the water play at different time, such as large and heavy things that float; small things that sink; a variety of materials, including woods, metals, plastics; and things that absorb water like cloths, sponges and chalk. As far as possible, however, objects that rust or have sharp edges should be avoided. The children need to observe carefully what happens when the objects are put into the water. Skilful questioning by the teacher will improve the quality of observations. Did the sinkers sink straight away? Did they take a long time to get to the bottom? What are slow sinkers like? How did the object move in the water? Does anything come out as it sinks (air)? What do floaters feel like? Which way up do they float? How do they move about on the water? What happens when you blow or splash gently? The children can also be encouraged to ask each other questions and to suggest criteria for setting the objects.

After a time of informal observation, talk and perhaps recording, the children's attention can be focused on the factors that influence flotation. It is important to start with the children's idea about flotation. A variety of objects that include things that might not act as the children expect will stimulate questions and thought. These might include an apple, a corked glass bottle, a tennis shoe, a brick, a feather, a blown-up balloon, an empty tin with a lid, and a full baked bean tin. The children can initially be asked to guess whether the object will float or sink before trying it in the water. Children are usually very keen to please the teacher by getting the 'right' answer so that it is very important to reassure children that predictions do not need to be right. It is the normal scientific procedure that enables scientists to make a hypothesis which can then be tested. Scientists are just as interested when their prediction is incorrect as they are if it is shown to be correct.

Having made their predictions the children can then test the objects. Their observations and comments will indicate what further activities need to be provided. If they say all heavy things sink, they should sort out a set of heavy things and a set of light things and test them. If they suggest hard things sink, a similar sorting and testing activity can be carried out.

A more open-ended problem will provoke further thought. Can they make floating things sink? Or can they make sinking things float? Floating things can be made to sink by being weighted down, by having any air inside them removed or by being filled with water. For example, open containers will sink if turned upside down; a bottle will sink if filled with water; and wood will sink if enough weights are added. Things that would normally sink can appear to float by adding air to them, e.g. a paper clip can be held up with a balloon. A sinker will seem to float by placing it on to something that already floats, like a piece of wood. This type of activity enables the children to start to appreciate that air content is an important factor.

The importance of shape is not normally obvious to children. If they are given plasticine and asked to make it float they are likely to think the task is impossible. With trial and error they will discover that making the plasticine very thin and flat or boat-shaped will work. The problem can be extended by asking who can make their plasticine carry the heaviest weight. One-gram units are useful for assessing the boat shapes. Hopefully the children should now be able to appreciate how heavy metal boats float. At this stage it only necessary that children know that shape is important. Later they will learn that when an object is put into water two opposing forces act on it. Gravity pulls the object downwards, whereas the water produces an upthrust. There is more upthrust on a shape with a wide base than on a rolled-up ball containing the same amount of material (see Chapter 10).

Solids

Quite rightly, collections of interesting objects frequently feature in the infant classroom. Observing, classifying and setting for different properties are important activities for both early mathematics and scientific development. As part of general on-going activities very young children might make collections of a particular colour or shape or type of material. However, as they mature they should investigate properties and types of materials in more depth. When older infants and junior children carry out detailed study of properties, such as strength, hardness, flexibility and absorbency, the study is usually best included as part of a general study of a particular material. Fabrics, wood and paper are considered in depth as examples.

Fabrics

The children's interest in fabrics might be stimulated by someone's new clothes; a book about clothes; or from the children playing with dolls. A variety of clothes for dressing up or role play and dolls of different sizes and cultures for the children to use is helpful, as starting with real clothes rather than pieces of fabric helps the children appreciate that science is relevant.

The teacher might ask the children to consider the clothes that they are wearing. Can they describe them in terms of colour, texture, design, pattern, feel – itchy, soft, warm, weight and thickness? What are their favourite clothes? What is special about them? What do they wear for different occasions, wet weather, a party or PE? Why do we need different sorts of clothes? Can they suggest ways of sorting the clothes?

To study similarities and differences in more detail pieces of material can be provided. Small-group work enables every child to take an active part and to stimulate ideas through discussion. Each child can investigate at least one piece of material and describe how it looks in terms of colour, weave and pattern, how it feels and smells. Does it smell the same dry and wet? Rubbings help children to see differences in roughness and weave. Magnifying glasses and microscopes help to focus their attention on detail. Does their material tear, stretch, pull, crush or cut easily?

Is it opaque or see-through? One way of helping children to find out as much as possible is to put them in pairs and ask them to compare their fabrics and ask them to find as many similarities or differences as they can. Once having shared their observations, groups could think of different ways of setting, or classifying, the materials. The pieces of materials can be used to record the classifications. A collage to record these findings can also be used to encourage children to think about which materials glue easily, or which glues are best for different materials.

Ideally the child should be asking questions and setting out to answer them. Initially, however, the teacher will probably have to start asking questions and trying to answer them by simple investigations to demonstrate that questioning and practical action is acceptable behaviour.

It is important that the question or problem suggested has meaning for the children. After a wet play-time the children might be asked where is the best place to dry their clothes and which clothes will dry quickest. The children will probably make several suggestions. They can then carry out a simple investigation to prove, or disprove, their ideas. The children will need a lot of help to make their experiment fair. Only the factor they are testing must change. If they are testing the best drying location the type and size of material and the amount of water on each piece must remain the same. The pieces are then put in different places – outside on a line, on the playground, in a cupboard, on the radiator, on a desk – and felt after the same amount of time. As the children mature the measurements of time and water used can be more accurate.

Washing clothes might start another set of investigations. The children can consider which materials clean best. This can be assessed by rubbing equal amounts of dirt into different materials and then washing them. Other children might try to find the best way to wash material: using the same type of material with the same amount of dirt and washing in cold water, cold water with soap, warm water or warm water with soap.

A collection of gloves, perhaps abandoned in the lost property box, can initiate an investigation into which gloves are best. Before testing for the best material it is necessary to know what jobs gloves do. The children will probably suggest that gloves should keep hands warm and dry and look good. Other suggestions, such as they should also be good for catching balls or should not get lost, might also arise.

Having decided what makes a good glove the children can try to think of ways of testing them. If the teachers know at least one way of carrying out the tests they can prompt the children. The children may come up with an equally valid way. One way of testing the warmth of various materials is to wear gloves of different types and hold ice cubes in plastic bags and judge which are most effective. A more accurate method is to wrap several bottles in different materials. The bottles are then filled with hot water and the rate of temperature loss is measured by feel or a thermometer. The second method is rather abstract for very young children.

A similar activity can discover which gloves become uncomfortable when wet. Different gloves are again worn and about two spoonfuls of water are sprinkled on each glove and rubbed in. After a few minutes the child decides by feel which gloves feels most comfortable. If the gloves are then pressed on coloured paper towels wet side down it will be easy to see which glove loses most water, or has absorbed least. The children should discover that wool gloves keep hands both warm and dry very effectively as this is what wool does for the sheep. A general collection of gloves, e.g. gloves for gardeners, nurses, golfers and drivers, can develop into further discussions on the appropriateness of different materials for specific jobs.

The suitability of material for different types of clothes has a lot of potential for investigations. The children might be asked to find which materials would make the best raincoat, winter coat or summer T-shirt. An investigation of which materials are waterproof can be extended by asking the children to find a way of making non-waterproof materials waterproof. Different pieces of material can be stretched over yoghurt pots and held in place with elastic bands. A dropper is used to drip drops of water one at a time on to the material. The time taken for the water to disappear is measured. Ways of making material waterproof can be tried. White glue, wax, nail varnish and vaseline all work.

- Which materials are stretchy? How does the choice of fastening and openings of clothes depend on the amount of stretchability of the material?

  Cut strips of equal length and measure the amount of stretch when they are pulled.

- Which materials make the best towels, i.e. absorb water best?

  Hang strips of material in coloured water and see how far up the material the water travels.

- Which materials wear best?

  Rub sandpaper on to different materials and count the number of rubs to make a hole, or amount of fibre left on the sandpaper after four rubs.

- Which materials shrink?

  Measure the area or draw around the material before and after washing.

Young children or those with little scientific experience will need a lot of discussion and guidance before starting an investigation. Older children will need the challenge of thinking up their own way of carrying out an investigation fairly. Applying the knowledge they have learnt during an investigation helps the teacher to assess the children's understanding and enables the children to establish the concepts concerned. After work on textiles they could be given the problem of designing clothes to wear on a trip to a farm in November. The children should be able to choose appropriate materials and give reasons for their choice. Warm and easily cleaned waterproof materials, with appropriate fastenings for the stretchability of the material, might be considered. A collage or model is a way of recording their work.

Wood and paper

A topic on wood could be part of work on structures, buildings, the growth of trees, or how wood is processed and used. These studies will involve the use of secondary sources. Secondary sources are a valuable part of primary science to extend and develop ideas but should not be central to the children's study.

The children are usually surprised at how many types and uses of wood they can find in the school and its environment. A collection of wooden objects and small pieces of different sorts of wood could be made. Timber merchants often have off-cuts. As with the textiles the children could find as many similarities and differences as they can in terms of colour, size, shape, texture, smell, use and sound when tapped. Is the wood in its natural form? Do the colours vary? Is there a pattern? Can the children describe it? Is it made up of layers or tiny chips? Has the wood been treated? Has it been painted, varnished, sandpapered or carved? What happens when the wood is wet or put into water? If the children are given a variety of types of wood, including hardwoods, e.g. mahogany, and very light woods like balsa wood, they should find that they float in different positions in the water, depending on their density.

If a lot of scrap wood is available, groups of children can construct simple objects. They can select pieces and see how many different things they can make. Once they have decided which is their favourite they can try to find a way to keep it together permanently. If the teacher provides a variety of glues, nails, tacks, strings, threads, wire and hammers the children can discover how to fix the model by trial and error. Each group can then report about their model and what they discovered about the wood and best ways to fix it. If the children have not already had experience in handling tools, a project on wood provides a good starting point. With appropriate supervision even nursery children can be taught to handle hammers, nails and saws correctly and safely. Once children have been shown how to use tools, these can increasingly become part of the normal provision for the children's use. The ability to choose and use such tools and wood appropriately is an essential skill in technology.

Young children can learn to use hammers, hand drills, small saws, sandpaper, planes, pliers and screwdrivers. While studying how these tools are used to change wood it is also worthwhile looking at the design of the tools themselves. Can the children identify the materials used to make the tools and suggest why these materials are appropriate? They are usually made of wood and metal so that they are strong enough to cut, hit, make holes or smooth things without breaking and can also be held comfortably. Not all woods could be used to make tools because they are too soft. The children could try to think of a way to test pieces of wood to find out which are hard or strong enough to be used in a tool.

One way is to invent a scratch test. Each piece of wood is tested with a variety of implements which have different hardness and edge, e.g. plastic needle, pin, blunt knife, nail. Another method is to knock the same type of nail into the wood using a consistent number of taps with a hammer and measure how far the nail penetrates. Yet a third method is a dent test. In this case a heavy weight is dropped on the wood or it is hit with a hammer, and the hole produced is compared with those in other wood.

When the children were exploring the environment they may have noticed that wood is frequently used in building. Can they suggest why it is appropriate? It is used in roofs because it is strong and light. A test to find out how strong wood is can be carried out. The flexibility of wood is used in many objects, e.g. boats, bows and tennis rackets. Again the flexibility of different woods, lengths and widths can be measured. (See the experiments in Chapter 11.)

One disadvantage of using wood is that it absorbs water and rots. By weighing and drawing round a dry piece of wood and then again after soaking it the children can see how the wood has absorbed water and increased in size. They could also look at the effect of leaving the wood somewhere warm to dry. The children can be asked to suggest how damage by alternate soaking and drying can be avoided. They might need to look at how wood is treated outside. Can they suggest and test ways of treating wood? Will varnish, glue, school paint or oil keep out water?

Paper

By looking at paper carefully the children should be able to see the wood fibres that form it. If the children tear newspaper and examine the edges with a magnifying glass the fibres should be visible. Different types of paper have different fibre structures. In some papers the fibres are loosely packed together and will be more absorbent and tear easily, whereas in other papers the fibres are tightly packed and may have a filler, often china clay, between them. Good-quality writing paper is made smooth by plenty of filler. Different papers are designed and made to meet different uses.

The children can make recycled paper by tearing up the school's waste paper into very small pieces, adding water and glue as a filler, leaving it to soak and then mixing it into a pulp. The pulp is spread over a wire mesh, rolled flat and squeezed dry. If the children are mature enough the advantages and disadvantages of using wood or recycled paper can be discussed.

Studying the characteristics and strengths of different paper is very suitable in school because many types of paper can be seen in use there. A collection of different types of paper; glossy, speckled, thick, thin, translucent, coloured, dull, crinkly, stiff, carbon, cardboard, crepe, brown wrapping, wallpaper, corrugated, newspaper, hand towels and so on, can be sorted and classified in various ways. The teacher could discuss with the children how paper is used and what properties are needed, e.g. drawing, painting, printing, cutting, drying, keeping clean, wrapping, covering walls, etc. Having decided what properties are needed for a particular job different papers can be tested to find the best. Paper in a shopping bag needs to be strong; a paper towel should be rough, absorbent and be able to hold water when wet; tracing paper needs to be transparent; paper used to wrap something fragile has to be able to absorb the shock of bumps and knocks. Different groups could carry out different investigations and report their findings to the whole class.

One way of testing a paper's strength is to hang weights onto a strip and record the breaking point (Figure 2.1a). The absorbency can be assessed by hanging strips of paper into coloured water and measuring how far up the strip the water reaches (Figure 2.1b). Dropping drops of water on to paper stretched over a yoghurt pot and counting the number of drops it will hold before it breaks will show how strong the paper is when wet (Figure 2.1c).

Rough paper is needed to dry hands on but smooth paper is required for writing. Papers can be graded from one extreme to the other. The assessment could be done by touch or by putting a strip of Sellotape on the paper and then peeling it off to see how much of the paper's surface has been removed.

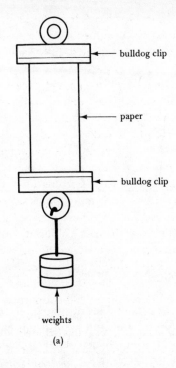

(a)

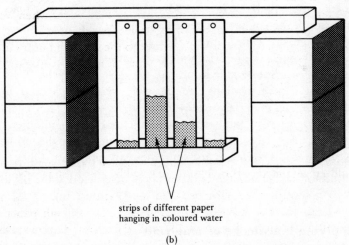

strips of different paper
hanging in coloured water

(b)

Figure 2.1 (a) Testing a paper's strength when dry (b) Testing absorbency

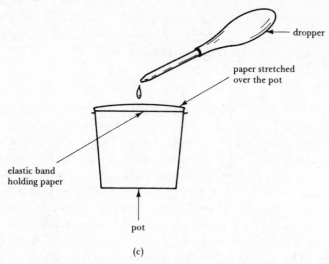

(c)

Figure 2.1(c) Testing a paper's strength when wet

Paper used to protect the tables during an art and craft session needs to stop inks, paste, glue and paint from reaching the table. Some children could test newspaper, kitchen paper, tissue paper, sugar paper and paper towels to see which are most effective and whether more than one layer is advisable. If white paper is placed underneath the paper to be tested and paints, inks and glues are dripped on, the white paper will be marked by those substances that go through. If the white paper is hardly marked the paper being tested must be able to protect the table effectively.

All these investigations are basically very simple and use equipment and materials readily found in the school. They enable ideas of setting up fair tests to be practised as the number of variables involved is limited. Also the children can see the test has relevance as it is related to problems they can appreciate. Once the children get the idea of such tests they will be able to suggest some themselves.

Applying knowledge of materials

Once the children have some basic knowledge of materials they might investigate an object or utensil to assess which is the best in terms of material and design. This type of activity has considerable overlap with technology. A study of spoons is one example that can be carried out by quite young children.

SPOONS

Spoons have many different uses, from a 5-ml medicine spoon to a large-bowled soup ladle. The materials used also vary widely, including plastic picnic spoons, wooden cooking spoons, silver carved teaspoons and metal dessertspoons. The children can set them in terms of material, use, size, durability, words, or marks or ability to reflect. The reason for using different materials to handle hot things can be simply demonstrated. If a metal, wooden and plastic spoon are all put into hot water, after a short time the children will feel the increased heat in the handle of the metal spoon. The teacher could also demonstrate how some plastic spoons melt when boiling water is poured over them. The advantages and disadvantages of different materials can be considered. Wooden spoons are relatively expensive to make but withstand heat well and are safe to hold; plastic is good for disposable spoons and handles but melts if too hot; and metal can be used when cooking hot things but becomes too hot to touch. Some materials are used to look attractive or to show wealth.

Once the children have some appreciation of the great variety of spoons they can try to design their own spoon, perhaps for getting individual Smarties out of tubes or a spoon for an unsteady old person to drink soup without spilling it.

Other artefacts the children could investigate in the same way include mugs, teapots, carrier bags and boxes for take-away food.

Further reading

Balding, B. and Richards, N. (1980) *Springboards: Ideas for Science*. Melbourne: Thomas Nelson.

Bennett, J. and Smith, R. (eds) (1984) *Bright Ideas for Science*. London: Scholastic/Ward Lock Educational.

Bird, J. and Catherall, E. (1976) *Fibres and Fabrics*. London: Macdonald Educational.

Department of Education and Science and the Welsh Office (1989) *Science in the National Curriculum*. London: HMSO.

Dixon, A. (1988) *Wool*. London: A. & C. Black.

Induni, A. (1981) *Materials in the Home. Level 1: Science Horizons 5–14 Scheme.* London: West Sussex County Council.

Jennings, T. (1989) *Wood*. London: A. & C. Black.

Kincaid, D., Rapson, H. and Richards, R. (1983) *Science for Children with Learning Difficulties*. London: Macdonald Educational.

Kincaid, D. and Richards, R. (1982) *Materials. Teacher's Guide and Cards.* London: Schools Council/Macdonald Educational.

Showell, R. (1979) *Teaching Science to Infants*: London: Ward Lock Educational.

CHAPTER 3
Investigations through the Seasons with Young Children

KEY STAGE 1
Traditionally most primary science has been based on studies of the weather, plants and animals. Teachers can extend this excellent base to develop skills related to experimentation. The children's interest in their surroundings can also be developed to help them to become aware of their responsibility to care for the environment.

The seasons and weather

Young children are required by the National Curriculum to observe and record the seasonal changes in the weather, plants and animals, and develop an appreciation of how weather affects people's lives. Older children should make regular and quantitative observations of temperature, rainfall, wind speed and direction. This chapter considers how young children can investigate some of the ways their lives are affected by different weather conditions through studying clothes and homes. It also examines simple activities they can carry out to discover some of the factors important for plant and animal life.

In many good infant classes children are taken out to observe the effect of the changing seasons on the environment around the school. Very young children need these opportunities to observe, describe and record the daily, weekly and annual changes in the weather and environment so that they can place later investigatory work in an overall structure.

It is important to develop both the children's observational skills and their natural curiosity by appropriate questioning. The children need to be encouraged to ask questions and to be helped to find ways of answering some of them. Initially the teacher will need to raise the questions to provide a model of behaviour for the children.

On a walk outside the classroom the teacher might draw the children's attention to moving things such as leaves, clouds and rainfall; prompt them to see differences and encourage them to suggest reasons for their observations. Do the leaves shake on different trees, bushes and plants near the ground to the same extent? How many clouds are there? Are the clouds the same size or at the same height? Do the clouds move in the same direction as the wind? What is the sky like when it rains? How do the raindrops fall on windows, puddles, soil, the playground and coats? These discussions may lead to the children asking their own questions such as where does water in puddles go, or where does the rain come from? Some of these questions can be answered by simple investigations and by reference to books.

By the time children are 6 or 7 years old they appreciate some of the characteristics of seasonal changes and are ready to explore how these affect people's lives through studies of clothes, leisure activities, eating habits or homes.

The children could collect pictures of different sports and sort them into those that are played in the summer, those that are played in winter, and others which are common throughout the year. They can discuss why some activities are appropriate for different weather conditions. Skiing needs snow. Football and netball are very active games that keep everyone warm. Cricket or rounders involves players standing still for long periods. People who sail or surfboard dress differently in different seasons but mainly require a good wind. Indoor activities such as reading and dancing are unrestricted by weather.

Eating habits vary according to the season. The children could paint or make a collage of meals they might have on a cold wet day or warm sunny day. They can discuss which items are to keep them warm or cool and which are related to food being available at that season. Typical meals of other countries could be prepared and discussed in a similar way.

A study of homes in different parts of the world can also prompt the children to appreciate how differences in climate influence how we live. It may be possible to supplement pictures, slides and videos of different houses by talks from children and parents who have had experience of living in different countries. The children can be encouraged to observe the pictures carefully and compare them with houses in Britain. If they think about how homes in Britain are kept warm and dry in winter, i.e. fires, double glazing, thick brick walls and sloping roofs, they might be able to explain why homes in Pakistan and India are often built with thinner walls, flat roofs and open windows. Investigations, suitable for older children, relating to controlling heat are covered in Chapter 13.

Clothes

Initially the children can consider how different clothes are suitable for different situations. This work might include clothes worn in different parts of the world. Mail order catalogues are a useful source of pictures of a wide variety of clothes. The children could cut out different pictures and group or set them in different ways. Ideally children should try to think of classifications for themselves. They may make suggestions which enable the teacher to discuss the significance of tradition and fashion as well as suitability for indoor or outdoor conditions. For example, the children may set clothes for different weather conditions; for men and women; for children and adults; or for western and Asian people. Subsequent discussions might consider whether these are sensible categories. Asian people often wear western dress and vice versa. Discussion of this type can introduce the children to the idea that although choice of clothes is closely related to suitability for the environment it is also influenced by historical developments, cost and personal choice. These latter ideas could be developed along the lines outlined in the National Curriculum for technology.

Simple stories such as Aesop's fable of 'The Wind and the Sun' could enable the children to start to link types of clothes with specific weather conditions. Dolls or a large cut-out outline of a child could be dressed for different weather conditions. The children could plan and set up a role-play area suitable for a cold winter's day that might include making model fires and lamps for the early dark nights. They could sort out warm dressing-up clothes and thick bedclothes and perhaps prepare and make soup. Another group at the same time or on another occasion could set up a hot day scene. If the children are involved in the planning they will become more aware of how different weather conditions affect many activities as well as being able to carry out a task that can cover all the technology attainment targets.

As part of these activities the children could carry out experiments to discover which clothes or materials are suitable for keeping people cool or hot. A very visual and tactile investigation for young children is to fill several hot-water bottles with hot water and then dress them in different clothes. One bottle could be dressed in a blanket; another in a child's coat; another in a T-shirt; and one left bare. The children then feel the bottles regularly over a two-hour period to find which items keep the bottles warm. With help, the children will be able to identify some of the factors that affect warmth retention, e.g. type of material, thickness of material, number of layers and whether air is trapped under the fabric.

The different factors can be explored by more accurate, but perhaps more abstract, investigations. The children could first look at the effect of using different materials. They should cover several plastic bottles in different materials, e.g. fur fabric, wool and cotton, and leave one uncovered. The bottles are filled with hot water, which is safe enough for the children to handle. The children should use an alcohol thermometer (not a mercury one, for safety reasons) to take the temperature of the water every half an hour to discover which fabric keeps the water warm longest. They can also feel the bottles, as they need the actual experience of feeling the differences in temperature loss to relate to the recordings shown on the thermometer. This activity is also valuable in enabling the children to learn to use a thermometer and to time experiments. Most infant children will not have had a lot of experience using a thermometer; if paper shapes the same size as the thermometers are provided the children can colour in the equivalent height of the alcohol each time they take the measurement, which will help them see how the level of the thermometer changes.

Once the children have carried out the experiment they can suggest why some materials keep things warm and can make hypotheses. They may predict that thick, fluffy or soft materials keep things warm. Different groups of children could test the different hypotheses with sets of thick and thin materials; soft and hard materials; or smooth and fluffy materials. The effect of having different layers of fabric can be tested in the same way.

Clothes for wet conditions might be investigated. A collection of things to keep us dry could be made, e.g. umbrellas, boots, raincoats and sou'westers. Pictures of people who work in wet conditions, such as firefighters and sailors, could be displayed. The children could also bring clothes they would wear on a wet day. If the children look at the labels on their rainwear they should find that some are described as showerproof whereas others are rainproof or waterproof. The teacher could discuss the differences between these terms and how they relate to different types of rainfall. The children could record how often showers, light rain or heavy downpours occur over a month to see how often a showerproof coat would have been inadequate. This could lead into discussions on the problems designers have in producing a coat that caters for many different requirements, such as attractiveness, comfort, warmth and protection from the wind, as well as being rainproof.

Once the children have looked at waterproof clothes the teacher could provide a variety of fabrics for them to predict and test which are waterproof. Each piece of material should be stretched over something like a yoghurt pot and held in place with an elastic band. The children use a dropper to drip water one drop at a time on to the fabric and count how many drops the fabric can hold before the water seeps through and how long it takes for the water to go through. Again, after the first experiments, the children should look at the results and make statements which they can test. One group might say 'All shiny materials are waterproof'. This is a valid generalization if all the shiny pieces they had tested had been waterproof. They could then make a new collection of shiny materials, which according to their statement will be waterproof, and repeat the test. They should find that some shiny pieces are not waterproof. A new generalization, 'Shine does not affect water-proofness', is now appropriate. By going through this procedure they have followed correct scientific method. During research all scientists make incorrect hypotheses, which after testing are re-adjusted and refined.

Fabrics can be made waterproof. The children could make suggestions and try them out on the materials which are not waterproof. They might try paint, glue, candle wax, nail varnish and polish. Although some methods will work they are not suitable for clothes because they make the material too hard to wear but they might be suitable for items like boots. This sort of discussion links with technology where the children need to realize there are often many solutions to a problem. The final choice depends on many factors such as use, cost, safety, attractiveness and ease of making.

An example of the conflict of use and safety can be illustrated by considering clothes with hoods. The children will be able to identify how hoods solve the problem of keeping them warm and dry, but can restrict vision and sound, making them dangerous when crossing the road. Different hoods can be tested. One child wears the hood and looks straight ahead. Another child moves a pencil horizontally around the first child's head, who reports when she can no longer see it. The angle of vision is marked on a circle placed underneath the first child. The children should discover that vision is far better without a hood. The loss of hearing when wearing a hood can be tested in a similar way. Again, one child wears the hood and looks straight ahead. The second child starts a long way behind the first and rings a bell quietly. As soon as the first hears the sound the distance between the two children is measured. Work on safety can be extended to look at clothes and materials that can be seen in the dark. The children could be asked to think of a way of finding out which colours can be seen easily in daylight or darkness.

If the school has children from a variety of cultures the children can be asked to bring in and talk about clothes from other parts of the world. After parents or children who have visited other countries have described the different climate, the teacher could encourage the children to suggest how the clothes worn are suited to the climate. Traditional clothes worn in India or Pakistan are designed to be cool by being loose and light in weight and colour. The design limits sunburn and bites by insects by covering most of the body. The children could follow this by testing the difference between white and black colours. Two bottles are needed. One is wrapped in white material and the other is wrapped in the same amount and type of black material. Felt is ideal as the pieces of fabric can be the same thickness and type. The bottles are filled with cold water and warmed with a hair-drier or in front of a heater. If the children take the temperature every half-hour they should find the black bottle heats up more quickly, because the white material reflects the heat. White clothes will be cooler to wear in hot countries.

Plants

Differences in climate, seasons and weather have a profound effect on animals and plants. There are opportunities to observe, collect and classify plant materials with every season. In autumn leaves can be collected regularly to compare the change of colour; date of fall from different trees recorded; twigs with different scar shapes found; and seeds collected and classified. Once flowers start to grow the children can record their colours and find the most commonly occurring colour each month. They might study flower shape and petal number and size. Leaves could be sorted into size, shape and type of edge. These types of activities help the children to appreciate not only the change of the seasons but also how plant life responds.

The children can study the plants in the environment around the school, perhaps have their own garden and have the opportunity to care for a variety of plants. This collection might include unusual plants such as cactus, climbing plants and Venus fly trap. The children could sort and classify plants in relation to habitat or use. The number of varieties to consider could be extended by using garden catalogues and other secondary sources. The children could group plants in different ways such as those that do or do not attract insects, are kept in gardens to look attractive or are weeds, are used for food, grow in water or live in hot places.

Children often have the opportunity to grow plants from seed in school. Classification and observation of seeds could be related. A wide variety of seeds could be given to the children, such as nasturtium, radish, lettuce, pea, bean, tomato, maize, marrow, wheat, grass and bird seed. The children can think of ways of describing and sorting the seeds. A magnifying glass will help them to see the fine details. They could then predict what will happen when the seeds are planted. Will big seeds grow quickest or produce the biggest plant after two weeks? Will all the seeds grow? Are some types of seeds more successful than others? All the seeds should be planted in the same way to make the investigations fair.

These activities will involve the children using the correct terms for the parts of the plants in a meaningful situation as well as giving them practical experiences of the similarities and differences of plants.

The children could also try to plant seeds in a variety of situations, such as on damp cloths, in egg-shells, in plant pots and in a jam-jar between the glass and blotting paper. It is important that children realize that plants can grow in many situations. Later they will discover that, although a plant can grow in many conditions, each plant's ultimate success in competition with others depends on the conditions or habitat being ideal for that particular plant.

It may not be obvious to young children that seeds of one type produce the same type of full-grown plant. If the children plant a variety of seeds this relationship should become apparent. They could also be given fruit or vegetables, ideally picked by them, to observe and remove the seeds for replanting so that they can see the link with the fully grown plant and the seeds. Although plants of one species produce mature plants of the same type there are small variations. This concept can be introduced to the children by giving each child the same type of seed to grow and compare. They could have a bean sprout competition. One Monday each child could be given five beans and on Friday have to find out who has the longest or shortest. This may raise another set of questions that can be investigated, e.g. do the biggest seeds give the biggest plants?

In autumn the children probably make conker collections. To use this initial interest, a trip could be made to collect a variety of tree seeds. The children could suggest different ways of setting the seeds. They could classify them into seeds that float through the air and those that fall straight down. The children may be able to suggest why this difference occurs, perhaps saying shape and weight are important. They could test whether weight is significant by dropping two balls of the same size but of different weights. They should find that these land simultaneously. They could try adding paper or cardboard shapes like those found on the seeds to a seed or piece of plasticine to test the effect of shape.

As seeds are not the only method of plant reproduction children should have the opportunity to see how some plants reproduce vegetatively. They could grow plants with bulbs or corms, e.g. onions, daffodils, bluebells and crocus; grow strawberries with runners; take cuttings from geraniums; or grow potatoes from tubers. A school garden involves the children in practical application of their knowledge. Peas, carrots, radishes and lettuces are usually successful and can be eaten by the children without much preparation. Flowers can be grown for sale or tree seeds could be grown for replanting in the park. Work related to the garden often interrelates with technology as this is a situation where scientific ideas are applied for human use. The decision what to grow is related to soil conditions as well as what the children like to eat or what they can sell at a profit at the school sale.

INVESTIGATING CONDITIONS FOR GROWTH

There are several simple investigations that infant children can carry out to discover what conditions are needed for successful plant growth. In these experiments a quick-growing plant such as mustard is needed so that the children do not forget the main purpose of the investigation. These investigations should give children plenty of opportunities to make hypotheses and to design and carry out fair tests.

Once the children have some experience of growing plants they may be able to raise further questions or suggest what factors are needed for germination and growth. These ideas can then be tested. Most children think soil is necessary. They could try different media, such as damp sawdust, pebbles, paper towels, cloth, sand, cardboard and sponges. To make a fair test the type of medium must be the only variable to change. The type and number of seeds and method of care must be the same for all.

Factors for successful germination could be tested. Is light, water and/or warmth needed? Does the depth of planting matter? Only one factor or variable should be tested in any one experiment, otherwise the children will not know which factor is influencing the growth. Different groups of children could try different investigations. Whenever possible the children should plan and carry out the investigation themselves. If they are testing whether light is significant they might keep one pot covered or in a cupboard and another in the light. These simple experiments which do not require a lot of equipment are particularly useful for introducing the importance of repeating an experiment. One example of keeping the seeds in darkness is not enough to prove whether light is important for germination.

Although the children should suggest a way of carrying out each test fairly, some individuals may rely on the teacher being able to prompt and advise them. One way of carrying out an investigation into whether depth of planting is significant is to use three small plant pots of the same size. Different groups could try different types of seed such as pea, wheat, barley or sweetcorn seeds. The children need to count out the same number and type of seeds for each pot, plant the seeds at the bottom of the first pot, in the middle of the second, and on the surface of the soil in the third pot. Each pot should be treated in the same way and the time and number of plants that are seen to start growing and their growth recorded. The seeds that are planted at the surface are likely to germinate quickly but many will not live long. Most of those that are planted at depth will not have enough stored food for the long growth needed to reach the light.

The importance of light for food and the strength of plants are important features that the children are unlikely to think of for themselves. In these cases the teacher may decide to raise the question or ask the children to set up an activity to observe and discuss what occurs. The teacher can prompt the children to notice how shoots and leaves turn towards the light and explain how plants need light for food. This can be demonstrated quite dramatically by growing a pea plant in a box with a lid and a hole cut in one side of the box away from the plant. The lid should only be removed for watering the plant. The plant will grow towards the light and eventually the shoots will appear through the hole. On another occasion the teacher could ask the children to plant three pots with about 10 pea seeds in each; to cut polystyrene lids to fit each pot; and then to put different weights on the lids, 100 gm, 200 gm and 300 gm. The seeds require regular watering but the weights have to be replaced after watering. The children should find that the lighter weights are pushed up by the shoots. Once they realize how strong plants are, they can look for evidence of their effect in the environment, such as creating cracks in pavements and walls. This is an important experience which introduces the role plants have in the weathering of rocks.

The effect of both light and gravity on plants can be seen by growing broad beans. Before planting, the beans need to be soaked overnight. The children are usually amazed to see how much heavier and fatter they are after soaking. Children who are not ready to use metric weights can weigh the beans against small plastic bricks. The children should place blotting paper around the inside of a glass jar with soil in the centre of the jar to hold the paper in place. Two or three beans are then placed between the blotting paper and the glass so that their growth can be seen easily. The shoot appears first and always grows upwards no matter how the bean is placed. If the children carefully move the bean so that the shoot is pointing downwards it will correct itself because shoots are phototropic, i.e. they move towards light. In the same way roots are geotropic and move downwards towards the pull of gravity. The roots also move away from the light and will try to push through the blotting paper into the dark soil. The children can draw or measure the daily growth of the shoots, leaves, roots and rootlets.

Young children tend not to assume that trees are plants. They are too big. However, this misunderstanding can be overcome by growing acorns or conkers in pots and then planting them in suitable locations or by observing and recording the changes of one tree through the year in a class book, and comparing its changes with the growth of flowers and small bushes. The tree could also be studied as a habitat for other living things; as the tree changes through the seasons the children can be encouraged to notice what happens to the related animals and plants. This also helps children to relate seasonal changes to changes in plant and animal behaviour.

Observing animals

Many teachers are experienced in giving young children opportunities to see and handle animals. These usually include keeping classroom pets, visits to local farms, pond dipping, feeding birds and keeping small wild animals, e.g. tadpoles, snails and caterpillars, for short periods at appropriate seasons. Investigations involving animals have to be limited because of the need to consider their welfare at all times.

The children need to have their skills of observation developed by being asked questions that draw their attention to different features, including movement, growth and feeding. If they observe an animal outside the classroom they should note where it is. Is it on the ground or at a higher level? Is it in a sheltered place? Is it in a dry or damp location? Is it on its own? Is it very visible or is it difficult to see? When the children look at the animal's movement they might be able to time and measure its movement or note if it moves too quickly to be timed. They should try to notice which parts of the body move and describe how and how often it moves. Does it walk, fly, glide, crawl, loop, swim or paddle? Do all the legs work together or in the same way? Does it move in a straight line? Does it rest in a special position? If the children have the opportunity to see the animal eat they can be asked what it feeds on and how it feeds. There may be signs of past meals that show what the animal likes to eat. If the children have collected some caterpillars they could be asked to watch them feed using a magnifying glass. Questions such as how the jaws work, or do the caterpillars eat by scraping, biting holes or chewing the edges, help the children to focus their attention. They can be encouraged to ask each other questions.

The children may also observe how the leaf is affected. If the caterpillar is only given one leaf the children can draw around the leaf in the morning and evening to see how much and what parts have been eaten. Asking the children to measure different things also helps them to observe variations and changes. If the children measure the caterpillar each day they should be able to find out whether it grows steadily or in spurts. Able children could record their findings on a graph. Less able children could cut out equivalent lengths or caterpillar shapes for each day. The data produced by different children may show a pattern, e.g. do all the caterpillars grow steadily? Finding a pattern in data enables scientists to make a hypothesis which can then be tested. If the children find all their caterpillars grow in spurts they can make a statement that 'all caterpillars grow in spurts'. They can then predict that a new caterpillar will follow the same pattern. If they find another caterpillar they can test this.

With care, the children can carry out some investigations into the food or habitat preferences of different animals. If the children have been observing earwigs or earthworms they may have noticed that they are usually found in dark places. They could then devise a test to find out whether earwigs do actually prefer dark places. The children may suggest that the earwigs are put into a large container, half of which has been covered with black paper. Later the container is checked to see where the earwigs are. A similar investigation could test whether earthworms or earwigs prefer damp places by putting a damp paper towel on one half of the container and a dry paper towel on the other half. After the experiment the animals should, of course, be returned to where they had been found. Food preference can be tested by providing the animal with a variety of foods to see which are taken. It is important to ensure the animal does have some food that it normally eats and nothing harmful is included. A class gerbil could be given a weighed amount of apple, potato, carrot and cheese. After a day the food can be re-weighed and note made of signs of eating. Squares of the same size from different leaves, such as cabbage, lettuce, oak, nettle and sycamore, could be left with some slugs. The amount of leaf eaten will indicate the slugs' food preference. The children may notice that the slugs are less likely to eat leaves that have come from trees, and could test this idea further with a different range of leaves. If the school is regularly visited by birds, different foods can be put out. Children could put out equal amounts of different seeds, berries, bread, crisps, fat and apples, and observe which birds take the food or note what food has gone. (Please note that it is inadvisable to put out peanuts during the spring and summer because they can be harmful to young birds.) A test to find out whether different background colours affect the feeding habits of birds might be done. Birds may prefer to eat from colours that reflect their usual habitat. To ensure that the test is fair the same amount and type of food should be placed on squares of different colours.

Caring for and improving the local environment

As part of their studies of the changing natural environment it is important that the children appreciate the need for its care. Young

45

children are expected to know that human activities produce waste products, some of which, but not all, decay naturally. They could use this knowledge to help to improve the appearance of their immediate environment.

Initially the children need to identify what waste products are produced, to what extent there is a problem, and consider what can done to reduce it. This is a topic which is closely related to technology, so there are many opportunities to tackle technology activities alongside the scientific work. These could include surveys of opinion and other people's actions; assessing the effect of posters; designing and making devices to collect litter; reviewing the design and purpose of packaging; considering the organization of refuse collection; as well as collecting data about litter in the area with a view to planning and carrying out improvements.

A survey of the waste produced by the children's own class can start them thinking about the quantity and content of waste materials. Different groups could weigh and sort the rubbish produced each day. Children sorting rubbish should wear plastic gloves and wash their hands after the activity. If they estimate the weight before weighing they will be helped to develop a mathematical appreciation of weights and may begin to realize that waste is very bulky but not necessarily heavy. Having weighed the rubbish they can decide how to sort it and then weigh the sets produced. They may decide to sort with respect to the original use of the item, such as sweet papers, crisp packets, papers and cans; or into type of material, such as plastic, metal, paper and glass. Over a week the results of different days can be compared. Whenever possible the children should be involved in deciding how to collect, record and present their information.

The survey can be extended to compare the type and amount of rubbish produced daily by different classes, the secretary, head-teacher, staffroom, kitchens and from the school grounds. The children could also ask their families to record on a chart what they throw away in one day. After analysing the data they have collected to compare litter from the various places the children may be able to suggest reasons for the differences. These explanations, or hypotheses, can be assessed by interviewing the teachers and children of the other classes.

The children will quickly realize that a huge amount of waste is generated daily. The class could study what happens to all the rubbish and consider ways of reducing and re-using the waste. The caretaker and cleaners may be prepared to be interviewed to discuss their jobs, to explain how the rubbish is collected, and how the children might help with keeping the environment of the school clean and attractive. Videos, slides and other secondary material will be needed to explain what happens to the waste after it leaves the school.

Ways of reducing waste include more economic use of materials and some kind of re-use. One group might sort through a day's waste to report on whether it could have been used more economically. They may find paper thrown away that has been only partly used, which could be kept for rough work; or after craft work examples of where a large piece of card has been used to cut out a small shape. Another group could interview the school cook, record what food is thrown away and carry out a survey of the children's preferences in order to make suggestions on how to reduce food wastage. They might suggest and design a poster encouraging children to finish their dinners or ask the cook to provide more of a particular food item, as long as it was suitably nutritious. Yet another group could look at and report on packaging. They could find out what items are typically packed in glass, cardboard, cans and plastic and suggest why. They could also look at unnecessary packaging where the package is much bigger than its contents or where one item has been unnecessarily covered in two or three wrappings, e.g. a drink carton wrapped in plastic. From this experience the children could design and make a sweet container for 10 sweets that is both attractive and uses cardboard economically.

Many children will know that some materials can be recycled, as most authorities have facilities to collect glass bottles, aluminium cans or paper. The many possibilities for recycling can be brought to the children's attention in an interesting way if they recycle different materials found in the school for themselves. They could be challenged to re-use a day's rubbish to make a picture or model. Old boxes could be used for a variety of models, paper could be used to make papier mâché, different coloured papers and scraps used for a collage, and recycled paper made and decorated. The recycled paper could be compared with commercially recycled paper and other papers. Discarded vegetables could be made into a compost heap and used to fertilize a garden area. Old clothes could be collected for fabric pieces to use in art and science, to keep for children who tear or get their own clothes dirty during the school day, or to be given to a charity.

Litter is an additional problem of waste. The children may not understand why it is so unacceptable. The eyesore it produces is fairly obvious but the children may not realize that small animals are often trapped and die in discarded bottles; pieces of broken glass and cigarette ends may start fires; and disintegration takes a very long time. The children could place different materials – leaves, paper, glass, a metal tin and plastic – in separate net bags and hang them in the open air, and then record the condition of the bags' contents weekly. The children will discover that paper, leaves and cardboard will disintegrate but do so very slowly. The metal tin will rust but is unlikely to change further in the time the children observe the bags; and the glass and plastic will be virtually unaffected. Consequently the children should be able to appreciate that if litter is left lying around it is not going to disappear quickly unless someone picks it up.

The children could carry out a survey of litter in the school grounds by collecting litter at different times of day to find out when and what type of litter is dropped. The location of most litter could also be marked on a simple map. The children should try to explain their findings. Is more litter found near where most children play, around the litter bins or in places where there is no bin, or where the wind blows it? They may be able to think of a way of testing their explanations. If the children suggest that most litter is found around the bins because it blows out they could make a lid for the bin and observe again. They could make a survey on days when the wind is blowing in different directions and when there is no wind to test whether the wind is important. Once they think they have identified the reasons litter occurs, they can try different ways to reduce it. They could design litter-collecting devices and clean up a particularly poor area in or near the school. These devices could be types of scoops or pincers on a stick to reduce bending down. Eye-catching litter bins designed to stop litter blowing out but also easy to empty could be made and posters encouraging people not to throw litter produced. As part of technology these solutions could be reviewed, improved and evaluated. The effect of the posters and bins can be tested by comparing litter surveys before and after their introduction.

If the children appreciate some of the variations between living things; know some of the factors needed for life; have some idea how animals and plants vary according to the weather and seasons; and are aware of the need for care and consideration for the immediate environment and all living things no matter how small or unattractive, they will have an excellent foundation which can be built on when they study different habitats in greater detail later in their primary schooling.

FURTHER READING

Collis, M. (1974) *Using the Environment: 1. Early Explorations.* London: Macdonald Educational.

Collis, M. and Kincaid, D. (1982) *Learning Through Science: All Around.* London: Macdonald Educational/Schools Council.

Department of Education and Science and the Welsh Office (1989) *Science in the National Curriculum.* London: HMSO.

Jennings, T. (1988) *Into Science: Earthworms.* Oxford: Oxford University Press.

Jennings, T. (1989) *Into Science: Slugs and Snails.* Oxford: Oxford University Press.

Kincaid, D., Rapson, H. and Richards, R. (1983) *Science for Children with Learning Difficulties.* London: Macdonald Educational.

Mares, C. *et al.* (1988) *Our Environment: Teacher's Guide.* Walton-on-Thames, Surrey: Thomas Nelson.

Mares, C. *et al.* (1988) *Our Environment: Workcards.* Walton-on-Thames, Surrey: Thomas Nelson.

Parker, S. (1973) *Minibeasts.* London: Macdonald Educational.

Showell, R. (1979) *Teaching Science to Infants.* London: Ward Lock Educational.

49

CHAPTER 4

Discovering Energy and Forces in Play

KEY STAGE 1
The National Curriculum requires that young children start to identify forces and energy in the context of their immediate environment and experiences. They need to begin to appreciate how simple devices move and store energy and to experience forces which 'push, pull, make things move, stop things and change the shape of objects'. A study of toys is an ideal way to start.

Describing and classifying toys

If the school does not have its own collection of moving toys the children will probably be able to bring toys from home. These toys might include cars, balsa wood aeroplanes, puppets, remote control machines, toy food-mixers, wind-up animals or boats and jumping animals on springs. The range should include a variety of power sources and toys that normally appeal to girls as well as boys.

The toys can be introduced to the children in several ways. The children might be given a toy in a pillow-case and asked to feel it and try to describe what is inside. They might be asked to talk or write about their favourite toy. A fiction book about a toy might initiate the work. Once the children have had a chance to talk about toys in general and have some idea how to approach ways of describing them, pairs of children could be given a toy and asked to investigate it.

If the toys have not always been available in the classroom, the children will need a period of fairly unstructured play with their toy before they are able to concentrate on investigating it formally. Periods of play of this type are often necessary when new material or equipment is presented to the children. The children are then able to make better use of the equipment as they can concentrate on a specific task and have begun to realize the toy's properties, potentials and limitations.

The children can be encouraged to talk about their toy's shape, size, power source, how different parts move, who usually plays with it and where. Some toys are modelled on animals. In these cases the children might compare them with the real thing. For example, do real mice move like a clockwork mouse? The children may need to be prompted to ask questions for themselves about the toy and attempt to answer them. They might try to find out how far a clockwork toy runs on one, two and three turns of the key. A spring toy with a sucker might initiate an investigation to find out how long it takes for the sucker to dry out to enable the toy to jump. Was it the same on each occasion? What was the longest and shortest time? How high does it jump? Such activities involve the children in working out how to time and measure the action of the toy. Children are usually very careful with their measuring because they are interested in the outcome. Science activities are frequently opportunities for children to apply mathematical concepts in a meaningful context. Once the children have investigated their toy they could prepare a spoken report for the rest of the class. This not only develops their oral skills but also helps them to clarify and order their ideas.

The children could also look at the whole set of toys and be asked to classify or 'set' the toys in various ways. They will come up with many suggestions: big toys and little toys; pretty toys; water toys; different colours; and toys with batteries. The teacher could take this opportunity to point out that some classifications are more useful than others. As different children will think different toys are pretty, this is too subjective. At what point is a toy big? Sometimes measurements are needed in classifications. If the children do not suggest sets related to energy sources the teacher can introduce them. The children could sort toys that move by pulling, pushing or twisting; or that move by using muscle power, battery, elastic or springs; or that store energy in an elastic band, clockwork mechanism or battery· or that move up and down, in a straight line, in circles, or in and out. The range of toys to be sorted can be extended by using pictures in catalogues, although these are no substitute for the real things.

Once the children are confident about applying the vocabulary of 'twist', 'turn', 'push' and 'pull', the topic can be extended to investigate how wheels enable things to move easily and to explore different energy sources such as wind, elastic, water and electrical power.

Looking at wheels

The children's attention could be drawn to wheels by going on a 'wheel hunt' and by collecting objects and pictures with wheels, e.g. toy cars, prams, wheelbarrow, clock, bicycle and the caretaker's trolley. As the children may only think of examples that are forms of transport the teacher may need to point out that the insides of other machines often have wheels. The children could try to find out how the wheels help each device to work and suggest ways of setting the machines. Their classifications could be recorded in a book. One book might illustrate objects with one, two, three, or more wheels and another might be about wheels found outside compared with those found inside school.

The problem of moving a very heavy box of books for the caretaker might be presented to the children. It is important that the children realize there is usually more than one answer to such problems. They might suggest pulling it with a rope, fixing wheels underneath or using rollers. A series of pictures showing how things were transported in history could be presented to the children for them to discuss how they worked and in what historical order they might have occurred.

Children from an older class or the teacher could make carts with strange-shaped wheels, e.g. square, triangular, oval and hexagonal; and with wheels of different sizes or with their axles off-centre. After predicting how each cart will move the children can try them out. The experience should enable the children to realize that a central axle and round wheels are essential for effective movement.

The children could now be asked to design and make their own moving car which moves by being pulled or pushed. A large variety of materials will be needed, such as cardboard boxes, wood, garden canes, dowelling, cardboard rolls and a variety of fastening materials, e.g. staples, glue and tape. In problem-solving activities of this type the children are likely to have more ideas if the materials are easily seen and available. Working in pairs or in very small groups also helps to develop their ideas and language. However, if the size of the group exceeds the number of tasks that can be genuinely shared, some children may not participate fully. Activities of this type take time, perhaps a whole day, to enable the children to plan, identify mistakes, solve problems and evaluate their work. However, such tasks are easily justified as they also cover many other areas of the curriculum such as written and oral language, technology and mathematics.

Making toys that show different energy sources

Making and testing toys enables the children to appreciate different energy sources and how energy can be stored. Several ideas are suggested, which vary according to the dexterity needed and the complexity of the instructions. The simpler activities are suitable for 6- to 7-year-olds. The children can be shown an example of the model they are to make or given instructions to follow; older infants or juniors can be set an open-ended problem of making a device that works by using a particular energy source. Following a 'recipe' for a model involves very little science unless there is some element of testing different variables or a problem to solve which enables the teacher to discuss aspects such as energy, forces or friction.

Windmills

If the children are given the instructions to make a windmill they could be left to discover that the paper sails will rub against the stick, thus stopping movement (Figure 4.1). This provides an early experience of forces, in this case friction, that reduce movement. The problem can be solved by putting something like a bead between the sail and the stick. Once the windmills are made, the children can try to find different ways of making them turn. They might suggest blowing, holding them in the wind, or waving them through the air, all different ways of creating movement of air.

Windmills

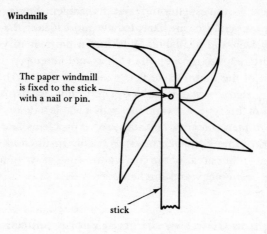

The paper windmill is fixed to the stick with a nail or pin.

stick

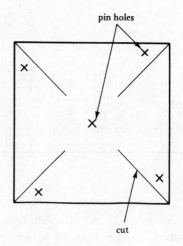

pin holes

cut

Figure 4.1 Windmills

Kites

Once the children have seen and perhaps had a chance to fly a kite, they could be asked to design and make their own kite using newspaper, polythene or thin cloth, dowel, string and paper. They can test their kites and discuss why some fly but others do not, and then make adjustments. They might consider the weight of the kite; the length of the tail; how long it stays in the air; how it is held up in the air; and what would happen in a strong wind or no wind at all.

Parachutes

The children could be asked to make a parachute for a doll or teddy-bear using different materials and different-sized canopies.

Gliders

Children who have not made folded-paper gliders will need an initial demonstration. Once they are able to make a glider they can try to make them more successful. The children need to decide what criteria to use in judging success, for example, a long distance flown straight. Watching the flight of the gliders should help the children to decide what factors make the best gliders successful. Why does one go further than the others? Why do some swerve to the side? The children may suggest that weight, type of paper, size and shape are important. With this information the children can plan, predict and then test new designs. Different kinds of paper (for example, tracing, sugar, tissue, foil) and simple weights such as paper-clips and plasticine will probably be needed. The task can be made more demanding for able children by asking them to aim to make their glider land in a particular spot or requiring the glider to turn.

Boats and land yachts

If the children are able to make a simple truck with wheels, they can try to make a land yacht which they blow along. Similarly, they can try to build a simple boat with sails (Figure 4.2). The size, shape and material for the sail can be investigated. The children will also need to solve the problem of providing stability for the yacht. They should discover that a big base or weighted 'keel' is needed. Activities of this type will provide a good foundation of experiences for the children to refer to when they study stability in more detail in the junior classes.

Boat

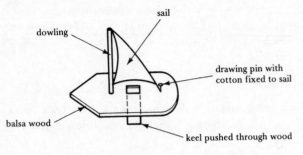

Land yacht

Figure 4.2   Boat and land yacht

Jet-propelled toys

The children could find out whether a large balloon goes further or faster when released than a small one. These models are also examples of released stored energy.

Toys pulled by gravity

Many children who watch television are familiar with the term gravity and know that things fall downwards because of the earth's gravity. This force can be used to make things move. The children can investigate this further by setting up equipment as shown in Figure 4.4. They might be asked to find out how many washers or weights are needed to get the lorry moving when it is empty and

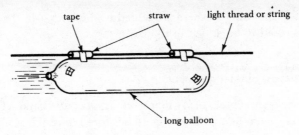

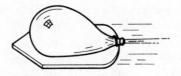

A boat driven by a balloon.

Figure 4.3 Jet-propelled toys

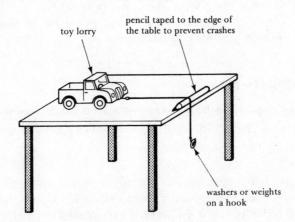

Figure 4.4 Toys pulled by gravity

loaded. If the same washers are added to the lorry will the same number need to be added to the string?

Toys using elastic power

There are several types of toy that work using elastic bands (Figure 4.5). Elastic bands enable energy to be stored until released. The children may also discover that the more twists they give, the longer the movement lasts, unless the device is stopped by catching or dragging on another part of the toy. In some cases this drag, or friction, needs to be increased and in others it has to be reduced. As the children make the model they will have to overcome problems, for example, the moving cotton-reel may not work because it slides on the floor. The children will need to glue rough material onto the cotton-reel to stop this. Later they will learn that rough material increases the friction and grip of a wheel.

If the teacher tries out the models beforehand, he can anticipate where problems are likely to arise and ensure that all the materials that might be needed are available. The actual models are quite complicated, so young children will need to be shown an example before they try to make one. Older juniors might just be asked to make a device that works using elastic power or be shown a diagrams which they have to interpret.

Exploring the park

A trip to a nearby park has great potential for studying forces. Most parks have a roundabout, swings, slide and a see-saw.

SLIDE

Once the children have had an opportunity to play on the slide the teacher could ask them to think about its design. What is the slide made of? What makes it slippery? What polishes the surface – is it rain or the children's clothes? Why is the slide initially steep and then with a gentle slope? Why are there edges to the slide? Why are the steps rough? How long does it take one child to slide down? Can they make themselves go quickly or slowly? Are heavy children quicker or slower than light children?

Moving cotton-reel or bottle

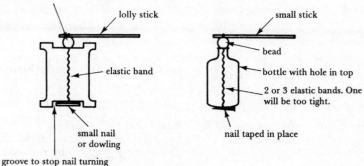

bead to allow ease of movement

lolly stick

small stick

bead

bottle with hole in top

elastic band

2 or 3 elastic bands. One will be too tight.

small nail or dowling

nail taped in place

groove to stop nail turning

Fairground roundabout

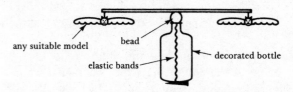

any suitable model

bead

decorated bottle

elastic bands

Boats

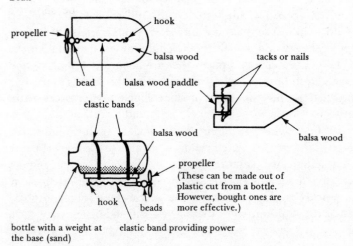

propeller

hook

balsa wood

tacks or nails

bead

balsa wood paddle

balsa wood

elastic bands

balsa wood

propeller
(These can be made out of plastic cut from a bottle. However, bought ones are more effective.)

hook

beads

bottle with a weight at the base (sand)

elastic band providing power

Figure 4.5 Elastic-powered toys

From questions of this type the children can be encouraged to come up with their own questions and to make simple generalizations, such as 'Things move quickly on a smooth steep slope but slowly when the surface is rough'. These initial observations can be extended by simple investigations in the classroom.

One activity is for the children to use a slope to sort things that slide easily from those that do not. The children should predict before testing and give reasons for their predictions, based on their experiences in the park. This activity can be extended by asking the children to sort objects into things that roll, things that slide, things that slide and roll, and things that do not move easily. If the children are provided with a variety of objects such as tins, boxes of different materials, weights, balls, marbles, toys with and without wheels, sponges, pencils, rubbers, rocks and pebbles, they can use these to decide what characteristics make a good roller or slider and why. The children can then try new items to test their ideas.

As the objects travel down the slope the children should try to notice what happens at the end of the slope; whether the object moves at the same speed all the way down; and whether the size, shape or weight of the object makes any difference to how easily it starts or its speed down the slope. Hypotheses can be made, based on these observations, and tested. The children need to be helped to set up a fair test so that they only change one variable at a time. If they say heavy things go faster than light things, they could make balls out of plasticine and paper that are about the same size and shape and test those. Another way of testing this idea is to use two strings tied so that the angle of slope is the same, as shown in Figure 4.6.

Different weights are hung on the hooks. If the weights are released at the same time the children are able to compare the rate of fall simultaneously (Figure 4.6a). A similar arrangement enables the children to see whether the same weight goes down a steep slope more quickly or slowly than down a gentle slope (Figure 4.6b).

When the children were playing on the slide they may have suggested that some materials slide better than others. It might be possible to try sliding on different materials, e.g. carpet, plastic and rubber. In the classroom they could try putting different objects, such as a piece of wood, rubber, ice cube and building brick, on

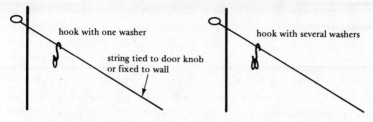

(a) Different weights travelling down slopes with the same angle

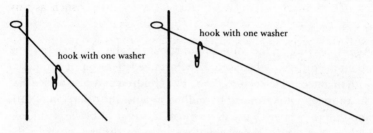

(b) The same weight travelling down slopes of different angles

Figure 4.6 Investigating the speed of objects down slopes

a slope together. As the angle of slope is slowly increased, the children will see some objects move earlier than others. After deciding what makes some things move easily they can predict what will happen to some new items and test them to see if their ideas were valid.

SEE-SAW

When the children examine the see-saw in the park they may notice that the movement is around a central point or pivot. Groups of children could be set different problems. Which children can always keep their end of the see-saw down and why? Which two children can make the see-saw stay level? Can they find a way of enabling a very light child to lift a heavy one, i.e. by the heavy child sitting close to the pivot? The children could try to find other things in the school which work in the same way, e.g. balances. Later in the children's school life they will learn more about levers, and early practical experiences of this type will provide a useful foundation.

SWING

Playing on the swing enables the teacher to encourage the children to notice how the swing starts; what body movements make it go faster; and what happens if the child's partner stops pushing. The children might also look at the materials and shape of the swing. If they try to make a working swing later they will probably discover that it needs to have a wide base for stability, and triangular shapes give the construction strength.

ROUNDABOUT

Again, playing on the roundabout should enable children to think about the difference between the effort needed to start it compared with that needed to keep it going. The children may also notice that the roundabout is stopped by pulling against the direction of turn and that they have to use their shoes as a type of brake. Children with smooth-soled shoes will find it more difficult to grip the ground against the turn of the roundabout. Later, when the children learn about friction and inertia, they will have experiences and observations to relate back to. At this stage they do not need to know these terms, but it is important that their observations and curiosity about moving machines is aroused. Hopefully they will also have started to suggest and test simple explanations or hypotheses based on their observations, such as 'rough surfaces slow down movement'.

The investigations related to work in the park could be completed by asking pairs or groups to design and build working models for a specific doll that were strong and safe enough for the doll. The doll could be weighted to simulate a child. Such activities will allow the children to recap many of the ideas already covered and to apply them in a technology project.

FURTHER READING

Ardley, N. (1984) *Action Science: Making Things Move*. London: Franklin Watts.
Balding, G. and Richards, N. (1980) *Springboards: Ideas for Science*. Melbourne: Nelson.

Catherall, E. (1983) *Elasticity*. Hove: Wayland.

Catherall, E. (1983) *Friction*. Hove: Wayland.

Catherall, E. (1983) *Wind Power*. Hove: Wayland.

Department of Education and Science and the Welsh Office (1989) *Science in the National Curriculum*. London: HMSO.

Fitzpatrick, J. (1986) *Science Spirals: Bounce, Stretch and Spring*. London: Hamish Hamilton.

Steel, P. (ed) (1984) *Bright Ideas for Science*. London: Scholastic/Ward Lock Educational.

Radford, D. *Schools Council 5/13: Science from Toys. Stages 1 and 2*. London: Macdonald Educational.

CHAPTER 5
Colour and Light

KEY STAGES 1 AND 2
The National Curriculum suggests that young children, in key stage 1, identify different light sources; explore opaque and transparent materials; and experiment with shadows and reflections. Although the children should learn to appreciate some significance of colour in the environment, an understanding of the properties of light and colour is considered more appropriate for key stage 2.

Early years

In the reception class these concepts need to be incorporated within other activities going on in the classroom rather than be given separate treatment. Teachers will need to be alert for opportunities to encourage the children to notice different sorts of light, colours, shades and shadows during play activities as well as indirectly in the more formal sessions. For instance, when taking a PE lesson outside on a sunny day the children might be asked to space themselves out so their shadows do not touch.

As the children get older the teacher will need to provide more specific activities designed to further their understanding.

Colour

Initially children need to learn to identify and name different colours. Many teachers already incorporate suitable tasks within art and mathematical activities. Understanding of the significance of some of these colours needs to be developed throughout the infant years.

The children can collect objects and materials for 'colour tables'.

These will give them some idea of the different shades of one colour that can be found. The teacher could ask the children to arrange the things in order from the darkest to the lightest in order to draw their attention to the considerable variation within one colour.

A series of 'colour days' excites the children's interest. For example, on one day all the children and teachers could try to come to school wearing something green. On that day different groups might make cakes with green icing; green jelly; and a salad with green vegetables, such as lettuce, cucumbers, green peppers, apples and grapes. Countryside pictures, underwater scenes and other green pictures could also be created.

The more able mathematicians can tally and record colours that people are wearing one day; and perhaps compare colours worn on fine and rainy days. Children can study one object and see how many different colours there are: e.g. a moss-covered stone, pebble or a piece of fabric. The children can to look for and identify colours in the outside environment, as well as inside the school.

COLOUR IN THE ENVIRONMENT

Colour in the environment can be part of several topics, e.g. on animals, plants or materials, or studied as a separate topic on its own. A separate science topic on colour in the environment has many opportunities to incorporate work of art and technology.

COLOURS IN THE STREET

The children could be asked to imagine that they are car manufacturers and have to decide on colours for a new make of car. Model cars could be made and painted as part of the project. The children initially need to consider what factors should be taken into account, e.g. which colours are most popular, whether some are more visible so are safer on the roads, what paints are available and their cost. After predicting what colours might be most popular they can try to confirm their predictions. They might make a tally of cars seen on the roads, ask other children and adults in the school, or even visit a car showroom to inquire there. Whenever possible the children should be involved in drawing up both the questionnaires and the method of recording data, as well as in evaluating their work. A decision will have to be made on the size of sample and the children may discuss whether 10 cars will give a sufficiently fair sample, or will 50, or 100, cars be needed. Will they need calculators to handle the large numbers? A small sample is unlikely to be representative. There may happen to be a lot of red cars seen at first and then no more for some time. A large sample will always give a more accurate result. The size will be limited by time and the computational ability of the children.

A test to discover whether some colours are safer for cars than others could follow (Figure 5.1a). Different coloured papers can be placed behind a variety of coloured cars to see which stand out best. Which cars will stand out against trees and hedges (represented by

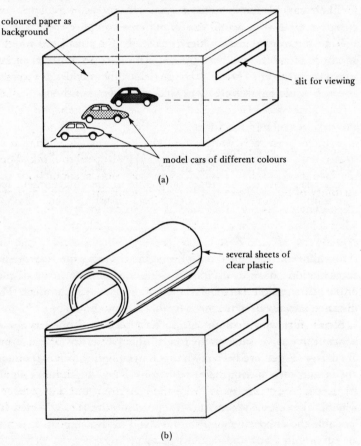

coloured paper as background

slit for viewing

model cars of different colours

(a)

several sheets of clear plastic

(b)

Figure 5.1 Tests to discover which colours are safer for cars

green paper)? Which stand out in the snow (white paper)? Which stand out in city streets (grey paper)?

The children could also consider whether some colours cannot be seen well in the dark and gloom. One way of solving this question is to replace the lid of the box with several sheets of clear plastic (Figure 5.1b). As the children raise one at a time they can make a note of which car is seen first, second, etc. Ideally the children are trying to identify a colour that can be seen well in all these places. However, if this is not the most popular colour, they should decide whether they will make their cars to cater for popular choice or to be the safest. They could also prepare advertisements for their cars referring to their research and scientific tests and compare them with actual advertisements.

Road signs have many different colours. On a walk around the neighbourhood the children can be encouraged to think about the use of these colours. What do the signs mean? Do they use words, symbols or special shapes? Which are most common? What makes a good sign? Signs in the Highway Code could be studied in this context. The children could design a sign, perhaps about putting litter in the bin or a 'Beware of the caretaker's dog' sign. They need to aim both to get the information over clearly and to think about the colours carefully. They need to take into account both the visibility of the sign and traditional conventions, such as that red often denotes danger. The children could devise tests to find out what colours are most visible for road signs, including the effect of putting two colours next to one another; does a combination of colours show up better or not? One way of testing the visibility of combinations of colours is to glue the same set of coloured shapes on to different backgrounds, then hold them up at the same distance and check which combinations stand out.

Street furniture (traffic lights, letter-boxes, litter bins and hydrant points) is often painted in significant ways. Some colours are designed to stand out so that they can be found, whereas others are intended to blend into the background. The children could locate and design a litter bin as a technology project and consider whether the colours should be bright and attractive to advertise its location and encourage people to use it or muted so that it is not an eyesore in an attractive environment.

COLOURS IN SCHOOL OR THE HOME

A collection of things used for colouring in the school will help to raise the children's awareness of the variety available. These might include chalks, paint, pastels, inks, crayons, dyes, etc. Such a collection will make the children more likely to consider their use in both art and technology as well as for sorting activities. The children should be able to suggest ways of sorting them. They might sort them into different colours; ones that have to be mixed before using; ones that can be mixed to get new colours; or ones that cannot be mixed at all.

A collection of wallpaper can be used to classify, collect, analyse and record data. Each child could choose one and say why it appealed to them in terms of pattern, texture and colour. They could sort the different wallpapers in different ways and carry out a survey to find the most popular, with a view to using it to cover their own books or to decorate a role-play area, deciding themselves how to measure, cut and fit the paper. They could even print their own wallpaper using large junk items, rollers and polystyrene, for printing.

As part of work on colours to decorate the home or school the children could investigate colour and mood. Do different colours make people feel differently? Different groups of children could be asked to paint a happy picture or a sad picture using only colour, shape or pattern rather than an activity or scene. The task could involve a survey to find out what colours make people sad or happy. This work could lead on to evaluating colour schemes used in the school and home.

Colours are often used to help sort and classify. For example, some schools colour code their books. The children could investigate whether a symbol for sorting books should vary in colour, shape or size. They could test this by using a set of Logiblocks and timing a friend who is sorting for different attributes. Which do they sort more quickly, colours, shapes or sizes?

People are part of the environment. Graphs or charts of hair and eye colour can be made, and the class might consider the variety of skin colour. It is possible to use this work to discuss stereotypes and differences within and between different cultural groups. To start the children questioning the simplified definitions of skin colour, they could paint a picture of themselves and try to mix paints to match their skin colour as closely as possible. They should find that skins are not pink, white or black. After having discussed what happens to some people's skin colour after they have been in the sun for some time, the teacher could point out that skin colour is a superficial insignificant difference related to the needs of different climates either to protect the body from ultra-violet light or to maximize uptake of vitamins from sunlight.

Food is a subject close to the child's heart and stomach. The children could investigate whether colour affects food likes and dislikes. After having recorded their favourite colour of a packet of sweets the children could be asked to see if they can accurately identify the colour blindfolded. Once the results have been collected it should be possible to see whether their choice was really related to the colour or the taste. They could write to a sweet manufacturer asking about colour choice. Similarly, the children could make up a packet of mashed potato and colour it with different food colouring; then ask others to taste it seen and unseen and make comments. Are certain colours less preferred, even if the taste is the same?

ANIMALS AND PLANTS

Birds exhibit a variety of colours which the children could investigate. A bird table can be set up to enable them to be observed. The children will find that colour is an important factor in their identification. If they look carefully even the plainest birds often have several colours e.g. a sparrow has black, white, grey, brown and chestnut feathers. An investigation to find the most common colours can be extended to encourage the children to question why some birds are brightly coloured whereas most are dull. Some are camouflaged whereas others are coloured to warn others from their territory or to attract a mate. Again, can the children suggest why the females are usually camouflaged but the males are brightly coloured?

The children can investigate whether birds can see colour. They could be helped to devise, plan, carry out and evaluate the test for themselves. One way is to colour squares of equal size and put out the same type and amount of food on to each square and record which food is taken. Some colours denote danger, e.g. red, and the birds may not be prepared to feed from these colours. Once the children's interest has been aroused by observations and investigations, they can use secondary sources to extend their knowledge and curiosity.

Bird and other animal camouflage depends on colour. The children's interest can be aroused by observing birds around the school or from fictional stories about camouflage. Some animals have a permanent colouring to fit with their environment; the stripes of the tiger blend with the light and shadows of the tropical grasslands, and the eyed hawk-moth looks like a dead leaf with its wings folded. Some animals change to blend into their background. The chameleon can change fairly rapidly, whereas the Arctic fox changes seasonally from brown to white to match the snow in winter. The children could use books as references to make and paint simple stick and cardboard puppets of animals, such as polar bears, caterpillars and giraffes, that are usually camouflaged. If the children then paint separate backgrounds for the animals, they can move their animals from one picture to another to see how an animal camouflaged in one environment stands out in another.

The children might invent their own animal. They could choose a place in the school or grounds for their animal to live and then draw, paint and cut out an animal that would be camouflaged for that location. They should consider the size and shape of their animal as well as its colour. After completion, the animal can be hidden in its habitat and another class or group could be invited to go on a safari. The children can be told that animals should not be killed on a safari but photographed and observed in their natural habitat. Obviously those animals that were discovered last were probably the most successfully camouflaged. Finally, some animals could be captured and a zoo built for them. This type of activity enables the teacher to discuss, with the children, when it is acceptable to take animals from the wild and in what sort of conditions they should be kept.

Other animals are deliberately conspicuous and are often red, black or yellow. These are warning colours that tell other animals not to eat them because they are poisonous. Ladybirds and wasps exhibit this type of colouring. Others, showing the colours of the first type, pretend to be dangerous to avoid being eaten, e.g. a hover-fly looks like a wasp. Children are fascinated by these animals, most of which have to be studied by using books or other secondary sources, but ladybirds can be caught and observed. The children's records of their observations could include models in clay or papier mâché. It is important that the children always return any living animal they have studied to the place where it was found.

Studying flowers is often easier than animals because they don't run away! On a walk the children can record the colours seen in order to discover the commonest one. Observations will be improved if the children paint or make pictures of the flowers with the aim to match the colour, as well as the shape, as closely as possible. The use of hand lenses enables them to see small details of colour, pattern or tone. Observation and questioning can further the children's curiosity. Can the children suggest why flowers have colours? Do they notice if any insects visit the flowers? What sort of insects come? Do certain insects prefer the same sort of flower? What happens to the colour when the plant dies? If possible the children should test their ideas by further observations as well as finding out as much as they can from books.

Light and shadows

Alongside the development of awareness of different colours and their significance in the environment, it is important to draw the children's attention to the variety of light sources. There are many opportunities:

- Songs and rhymes.
- Mathematical work on time; comparing day and night.
- Participation in festivals (birthdays, Divali, Christmas, Easter, Hannukah and Eid) when candles, fireworks, fairy lights, oil-filled divas or the moon are significant.
- Stories – including the creation myths for older infants.
- Lights used for safety – fire engines, police cars, ambulances, traffic lights and warning for road works.
- Guiding lights – street lamps, cats' eyes, lighthouses, airport lights.
- Work on shadows.

71

INVESTIGATING TRANSPARENT, TRANSLUCENT AND OPAQUE
MATERIALS

Different materials can be sorted into things that let light through and those that do not by shining a torch on to each item. If the children have a good variety of materials, such as glass, clean water, cellophane, clear plastic, lampshade material, frosted glass, fine curtains, paper, thick material, wood, stone, etc., they might notice three types of materials. Things we can see through clearly are transparent. Translucent materials will let light through but scatter it so that it is possible to see through them but only in a blurred way, e.g. frosted glass. Those materials that will not let light through are said to be opaque. Once the children understand the differenes they can explore the school and environs for examples of each type.

To reinforce the concept they might be asked to find the best windows for a doll's house, 'The Three Bears' or 'Three Little Pigs'. The children should discuss beforehand what properties windows must have and how they can test each material. They may decide to find out if the material is weatherproof by blowing on it through a straw to create wind and using a plant spray filled with water to simulate rain. They might test for transparency by looking through the 'window' at some writing. Each window must be tested in the same way. The children can cut out a house shape with windows like the one shown in Figure 5.2, and fix different materials, such as foil, net curtain, clear plastic and cotton cloth, in each space.

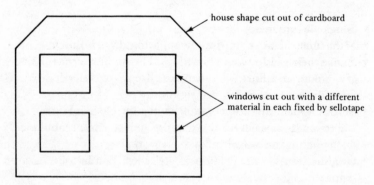

Figure 5.2 Finding the best material for a window in a model house

If the teacher asks the children to find a way of recording which windows are transparent and which let in rain and wind, they can try to list and collate findings and interpret these for themselves. It also demonstrates to them that more than one property has to be considered when choosing a material for a specific task.

The set of opaque things can be used to demonstrate that these make shadows when light is shining on them. When a torch is shone against a wall and one of the objects is placed in the beam, the shadow shows the place where the light cannot get past the object. The sun acts in the same way to make shadows.

SHADOWS

Shadow drawings can be made by holding up objects in the light and drawing around the outline of the shadow. Unusual shadows can be made by holding the object at different angles and other children can try to match the drawings with the objects. A torch or an overhead projector are useful sources of light.

A similar activity is to produce shadow portraits. One child sits sideways on a chair close to the wall. A piece of paper is fixed on the wall behind with masking tape. An overhead projector is shone onto the seated child so that the shadow of the profile is outlined on the paper. Another child quickly draws around the outline, which is then cut out. The children may need some help as they tend to be so careful that by the time they have finished outlining the seated child has moved several times, making a very peculiar profile. It fascinates the children to find that they can identify most of their friends' profiles.

Shadow puppets are very popular and have the added advantage that the subsequent plays develop the children's oral skills and often enhance their writing and reading. After listening to or reading a story, groups of children can prepare puppets to retell the story. As they get more advanced the puppets can have one or more moving parts, using a paper fastener and several sticks (Figure 5.3).

An overhead projector is ideal as the light source because pieces of background can be cut out and placed on its surface. With even more proficiency the children can add pieces of coloured transparent paper over cut-out parts of the puppet. These have the effect of giving colour to the puppet and using the property of

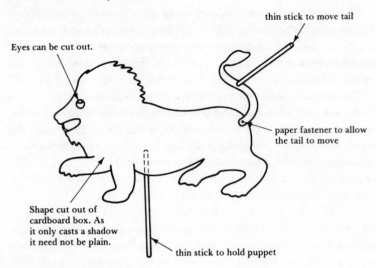

thin stick to move tail

Eyes can be cut out.

paper fastener to allow
the tail to move

Shape cut out of
cardboard box. As
it only casts a shadow
it need not be plain.

thin stick to hold puppet

Figure 5.3 Shadow puppet

transparency. Initially the children are often reluctant to tell the story and need the security of the teacher doing this while they join in at appropriate moments. As they become more expert with the puppets they should become more independent in reading the given story, preparing the puppets, working as a team to share the tasks, and acting and producing the final presentation.

When the sun is shining the children can be taken outside to play shadow games. The games will help them to realize that shadows change. They are sometimes short and fat, long and thin, clear or faint; and they are in different places at different times of the day. The teacher might set them various challenges: Who can make a long shadow? Who can make the shortest shadow? Who can make a funny shadow? The children can be asked to shake hands, observe their shadow and then try to make their shadows shake hands without the children touching. Can they move without their shadow moving? Can they hide their shadow? (In another bigger shadow perhaps.) In a small group can they make a monster shadow with several legs or an enormous body? The activity might be extended by giving the children an object to hold or use, e.g. a bag, chair, large box, umbrella or large ball, and repeating the activities.

After the session the class can recap what they have noticed or discovered. The children may be able to suggest why their shadow varies. It does not matter if their suggestions are incorrect; they are learning to make simple explanations, or hypotheses, which might be tested later.

Shadows can be recorded by drawing round them on the ground. If the shadow of the same child is drawn several times during the day the change of marks will show the sun's apparent movement across the sky. It is important to choose a site well away from a building which may itself cast a shadow over the investigation later in the day. The child's foot position must be clearly marked or they will tend to turn to face their shadow as it moves.

Repeating the exercise with another child on another day allows the children to predict what will happen and mark their prediction on the ground to see how accurate they are. Once they see a pattern in the movements they can profitably make a simple sundial. The shadow of a stick standing in the ground or fixed between heavy bricks can be marked every hour. Ideally the class should see a manufactured sundial and discuss the advantages and disadvantages of it as a time-keeping mechanism.

REFLECTIONS

Most work using mirrors is suggested as being most appropriate for key stage 2. However, younger children should have a short introduction to things that reflect light. Many children confuse shadows with reflections so it is wise not to deal with both concepts at the same time. If the teacher ensures that one concept is established reasonably well first, then there will be less risk of confusion.

If the surface of an object is smooth and shiny it acts as a mirror. The children should discover this by collecting things that give reflections: spoons, tins, mirrors of different types, kettles and saucepans. They could go on a reflections walk and notice taps, ponds, puddles, car mirrors, darkened windows, etc. Flat shiny surfaces could then be compared with curved ones. Spoons are particularly useful because the children can see how the reflection of their face changes on the two sides. The convex reflection makes the face seem fat whereas the concave reflection shows a small and upside-down face. Once they have studied a few spoons they could be asked if the same will happen on all spoons. In a similar way, after they have looked at several items, they can guess what their reflection will look like in other objects. Asking the children to predict helps to make them think about the reasons behind their observations.

PICTURES SHOWING LIGHT, COLOUR AND SHADE

When the children are recording their observations about colours and shadows they should try to include pictures showing light and shade by different ways of hatching pencil or crayon and by mixing different shades and tones of colours.

If the children, from an early age, are usually provided only with red, yellow, blue, black and white for art and craft activities they will become far more aware of how colours of paints mix. The children could investigate how many shades they can make using one colour and black or how many tones from one colour and white. They could also explore the effect of using different types of pencils and charcoal and try to record some shadow pictures using the techniques they have found.

KEY STAGE 2
During key stage 2 children should explore some of the properties of light and how it is affected by passing through different transparent objects, for example, lenses, colour filters, water and prisms. Children should investigate mirrors and shadows in particular.

The term light is commonly used in conjunction with light bulbs and/or differences in shade. Consequently the teacher will probably find that the children have a limited interpretation of what light is. They do not usually think of light as moving. Even when older juniors talk about light years and the fact that light takes time to travel they do not relate this to understanding that light in their immediate environment also moves over shorter distances and takes time to do so. As the children cannot see this movement or touch light, this is a particularly difficult abstract concept. The teacher's own usage, which emphasises that light comes from a variety of sources (using words such as sunlight and firelight) and has movement, will help the children to extend their understanding of the term. For example, when talking about shadows, the children may say the object is hiding the light. The teacher could add the idea that light is moving towards the object but cannot pass through it.

The importance of light

Radiation from the sun provides heat as well as light and is the source of energy for plants and, therefore, indirectly for us. There are other kinds of light beside sunlight and electric light. Some fish which live at great depth give out a luminescent light, as do a few rocks. Some types of light cannot be seen by human eyes. X-rays are one such example.

Much of the light which falls on things is 'bounced off', i.e. is reflected. Everything reflects some light. Some is reflected into our eyes which is how we can see. A shoe box with a lid, or similar box, is useful to show that light is necessary for vision (Figure 5.4).

If a child looks through the hole in the box, ensuring no light gets in, the mystery object cannot be seen. The class may be able offer several suggestions for what needs to be done. The object can only be seen if light is reflected off it, so a small hole in the side of the

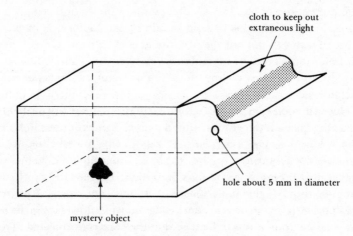

cloth to keep out extraneous light

hole about 5 mm in diameter

mystery object

Figure 5.4   Experiment to show light is necessary for vision

box will enable it to be partly seen. In order to see it clearly, more light is required, either from one large hole, which will scatter light around the sides of the box, or from several small holes, giving light from more than one direction. As this activity is likely to be a class activity, with only a few children having an opportunity to try the box, the others need time to try it out for themselves or to make a box for themselves.

The sun's importance for photosynthesis (the food-making process in green plants) can be introduced by experiments comparing seeds grown in the dark to ones grown in the light. Another way is to cover part of a leaf of a plant for a few days. The covered part will be much paler than the rest because it is unable to make food for itself. The children can make the pattern of their initials on a leaf by this method. Similarly, when the children are taken out to explore the biological environment, they can be asked why areas of plants or grass which have been covered are so pale in colour. Experiments demonstrating the attraction of plants to sunlight could also be carried out (see Chapter 3).

Under careful supervision the children can see how the sun's rays are strong enough to start a fire using a magnifying lens. If the children plan the activity to ensure safety, they are more likely to take care on their own. They will need to decide where it might be safe to carry out the experiment, i.e. well away from anything that might catch fire, what to burn and how to put out the fire should it get out of hand. A small amount of paper or dried grass placed in a metal bucket of sand should be satisfactory. A bucket or jug of water to put out the fire should also be near. One of the children should hold the magnifying lens over the crumpled paper and concentrate the sun's rays onto it. The resultant fire is put out with the water.

This is a good time to talk with the children about the dangers of leaving glass on the ground after a picnic. The children can also discuss how the magnifying lens, or glass, helps to make the fire. Some children think that because the lens is normally used to make things look bigger it must make the light bigger, rather than concentrating all the light reaching it onto one spot. A light box, borrowed from a secondary school, will show how a lens can bend narrow beams of light so that they are concentrated in a point.

The movement of light through different media

HOW LIGHT MOVES THROUGH AIR

Light normally travels in a straight line through air. It is not possible to see around a wall or corner. A simple experiment can be set up to demonstrate that light travels in a straight line. Each group needs four pieces of card of the same size, a torch, a knitting needle and plasticine. The centres of three cards are first found by marking where the diagonals meet and holes are made. The cards should be set up as shown in Figure 5.5.

The knitting needle is used to line up the cards in a straight line and removed. A torch is then shone through the holes and the position where the light falls on the last card is marked. When one of the cards is moved out of line, it will no longer be possible to shine the light through all the holes. The teacher can ask the children if they can explain what has happened.

Once the children understand that light travels in a straight line they should be able to use this knowledge to predict the position and size of shadows. A shadow box can be made to investigate shadows further (Figure 5.6).

Once the children have prepared the equipment they can investigate how the size and shape of the shadows can be varied. Some activities could be suggested to start the investigations but

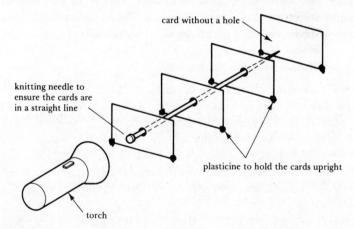

Figure 5.5 An experiment to demonstrate that light travels in a straight line

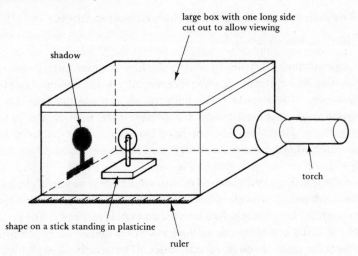

large box with one long side
cut out to allow viewing

shadow

torch

shape on a stick standing in plasticine

ruler

Figure 5.6   A shadow box to investigate shadows

the children may be able to think of additional problems. Some possible investigations include: Do the shadows get bigger or smaller as the shape is moved towards the back of the box? At what point is the shadow the same size as the shape? When the shadow is twice the size of the object, compare the distances in front of the shape to the end of the box and behind the shape to the light source. Using cardboard and plasticine make a variety of 2D and 3D shapes and draw the expected shadow before testing it. Predict what will happen when the shape is turned round.

HOW LIGHT MOVES THROUGH WATER

Light travels at different rates through different materials. A transparent beaker with straight sides, a cup, a straw, a coin and a jug of water are needed. The children should fill the beaker, put the straw in, look carefully at the straw and report their observations. The straw will appear to be broken at the boundary between the water and air. This is because light is refracted, or bent, as it passes from the denser water to air. Water also magnifies the straw.

Next, one child could place the coin at the bottom of a cup and slowly move the cup away from a partner until the coin is just out of this second child's sight, hidden by the rim of the cup. The second child should keep still while the first pours water into the cup. The coin will become visible. When the water level is raised light travelling from the coin is bent at a higher point and so reaches the eye. The children may be able to suggest where they can see this effect. They could look at a goldfish and see the difference between its appearance in the water and on the surface. The children might notice that their legs look thicker and shorter in the swimming pool and that it is very difficult to tell how deep the pool is.

Water acts as a magnifying glass, making things appear bigger. The children can discover this if they place droplets of water, from droppers, onto glossy printed paper and observe what happens to the print. The children could investigate whether each droplet affects the print in the same way? It is important that the children notice the shape of the water droplets. They are acting in the same way as convex lenses.

LOOKING THROUGH GLASS OR PLASTIC

A collection of transparent glass and plastic objects, such as bottles, glasses, glass from a picture frame and a fish bowl, can be used to discover how images are distorted by curved glass or plastic. If the children look at pictures or print through these objects, they should be able to sort the objects into those that make things look bigger, those that make things look smaller and those that do not cause any distortion, and then try to suggest what is common about each set. For example, the things that do not distort the image will be the flat, clear materials. Following this experience the children can test their ideas by using some manufactured lenses. These are transparent materials deliberately designed to change an observed image by bending light accurately. The children need the chance to work out the differences and properties of the lenses for themselves.

Convex lenses make things look bigger, e.g. a magnifying glass. Things look smaller through a concave lens (Figure 5.7). A collection could be made of things that use lenses: spectacles, binoculars, telescope, microscope and camera. The human eye has a lens but this is made not of glass but of a soft jelly-like substance.

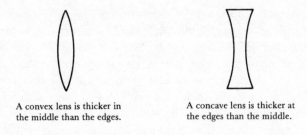

A convex lens is thicker in
the middle than the edges.

A concave lens is thicker at
the edges than the middle.

Figure 5.7 Convex and concave lenses

If the children look carefully they can see the bulge of the lens at
the front of our eyes. They could also look at pictures of other
mammals' eyes, which often bulge more than the human eye.

Reflection of light from shiny surfaces

It might be necessary to recap the work done in the early years
about reflections from shiny things. A collection of mirrors (e.g.
mirrors for cars, dentists, make-up and budgerigars) can be
compared and their different design discussed. The children can
be set the task of making a mirror. They might do so by covering
card with very smooth foil or they might try putting an opaque
backing on glass.

INVESTIGATING FLAT MIRRORS

Ideally the class should have a collection of mirrors of the same type
and size, since a variety of thick, thin, large and small mirrors gives
unnecessary variables to a child trying to think scientifically. The
use of bulldog clips attached to the side of the mirror, plasticine or
corks with slits enables the mirrors to be fixed vertically.

It is probably wise to allow a fairly unstructured time when the
children first get the mirrors as they will find them very exciting.
They can be taken outside when it is sunny. They can try bouncing
sunlight on the walls, play light spot tag, where one light spot has
to catch another, or make a light spot follow a given line along the
top of a fence or line in the bricks. These activities should start the
children realizing that mirrors reflect light.

Using a mirror enables us to look round corners. One child

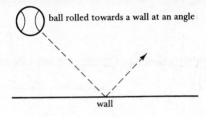

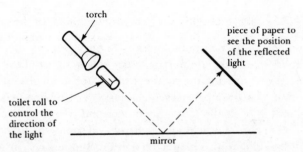

Figure 5.8 Investigating how light is reflected by a mirror

holding a mirror can sit out of sight of the others and use the mirror to say what another is putting on a table. Others can explain what is happening behind them, round a corner or over a high screen by using a mirror. It is possible to see around corners because the light is reflected by the shiny surface in the same way as a ball bounces. This can be demonstrated by the activity shown in Figure 5.8.

A very simple periscope is made by fixing a mirror to the end of a ruler (Figure 5.9). It can be used to look over tall obstacles. Periscopes using two mirrors are difficult for children to make because they involve sighting the mirrors at very accurate angles. A commercial one, however, would be very valuable to show them.

Children need to appreciate that mirrors reverse images. Using paint or ink the children could write their names and then place another piece of paper on top in order to get a print. These two pieces of paper can then be observed in the mirror. The teacher could also ask them to print their names while looking in a mirror. They should notice the reversal of the letters. They can be asked if they have noticed occasions when there is mirror writing in the

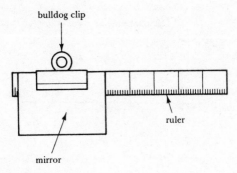

Figure 5.9 Simple periscope

environment, e.g. on ambulances. Playing games where the children have to make the mirror image touch a part of the face, e.g. the left ear, or wink the right eye also helps them gradually to realize that a mirror reverses the image. To further help this understanding one child looks in a mirror and performs an action while another child sits behind the mirror and copies the first child. The children might also play a version of 'Simon says' in which they have to follow the exact action, e.g. when one person waves her left hand, all the others have to wave their left hands. This game can be followed by one in which they have to mirror the action.

The children can investigate how mirrors change images in other ways. If the children draw a picture of a man and then place the mirror on different parts of the paper they can make two men or only half a man appear. Children can be set problems with provided pictures, for example, to make a longer or shorter stripe; to make two boats far apart or close together; to make a fat, thin ghost or make it disappear altogether. *Make a Bigger Puddle, Make a Smaller Worm* by Marion Walter has many ideas. Groups could make their own mirror books, with a home-made mirror, along these lines to share with others.

Investigating how to complete half drawings by using mirrors can lead on to investigating symmetry in general. The children could be given half a picture, e.g. a butterfly or ladybird, and asked to complete it using a mirror to help. The children could predict which letters of the alphabet will look the same in a mirror, and then check. Many mathematics books contain activities of this type.

(a)

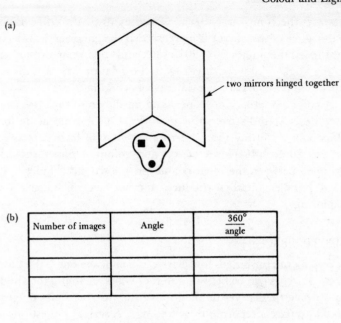

two mirrors hinged together

(b)

Number of images	Angle	$\dfrac{360°}{\text{angle}}$

(c)

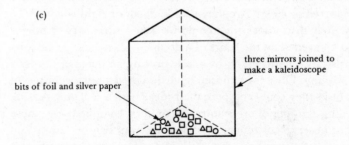

three mirrors joined to make a kaleidoscope

bits of foil and silver paper

Figure 5.10 Investigating reflections in two or more mirrors

Using two mirrors leads to another set of investigations. After hanging two mirrors together like a book with masking tape (Figure 5.10a), the children can investigate what happens to the image of an object placed between the mirrors. It is better to use something small and not symmetrical. Similarly a pattern made with sticky shapes could be placed in front of the two mirrors. Questions help to focus the children's attention onto details. How many times is the pattern repeated? Which way round is it? What shape is the complete pattern? Can they draw it? What happens if the angle of the mirror is increased? If the children draw a circle and mark the angles 60°, 90°, 180° and then match the mirrors to the angles, they can investigate the relationship of number of images and angle between the mirrors (Figure 5.10b).

A commercial kaleidoscope could be shown to the class so that they can try to discover how it works. One can be made in the classroom by fitting three mirrors together to form a triangular prism. Some tiny pieces of foil and coloured paper should be dropped between the mirrors and moved around (Figure 5.10c). Two parallel mirrors produce another set of images worth exploring.

CURVED MIRRORS

A convex mirror bulges towards you, a concave one bulges away. Some mirrors can be bent in different ways, enabling the children to observe themselves as they move the mirror. Pairs or groups could prepare a report of their findings. A series of questions may help to start their investigations. How big do they look? Do they look blurred or clear? Are they upside down or right way up? To apply their discoveries they could be asked what sort of mirror would be needed on the stairs of a double-decker bus; on cars; by a dentist; by a hairdresser; by a lady putting on make-up; or by a man shaving. Once the children have designed a mirror for one of these tasks they could compare their ideas with a real one. A book recording sighting of other mirrors could be compiled, e.g. those used to observe customers in shops, mirrors behind lamps and torches to reflect the light outwards, and mirrors on Christmas tree decorations. As an applied technology problem the children could be asked to make a mirror to do a specific task, such as enable the reception teacher to observe how many children are in a playhouse.

Coloured lights and coloured paints

Sunlight looks white but it is actually made from seven different colours, called the spectrum. The colours of the spectrum are red, orange, yellow, green, blue, indigo and violet. The children can create their own rainbows by using a triangular glass prism and

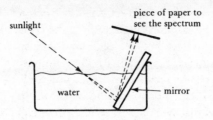

Figure 5.11   Making a rainbow using a mirror

holding it up in the sunlight. The spectrum should appear on the wall or ceiling. Blowing bubbles is another way to see the spectrum. (Bubbles are also an excellent stimulus for poetry.) Yet a third way is to place a mirror in a shallow box of water in sunlight (Figure 5.11).

The colours of the spectrum are bent different amounts by the water or prism and so are sorted out. The white rays of sunlight fall on drops of rain, which act in the same way as the prism to form a rainbow. A rainbow does not really have two ends that touch the earth but is a circle, which can be seen from an aeroplane or mountain top.

All the colours of the rainbow can be made from three coloured lights called primary colours. The primary colours of light are red, green and blue. They are not the same as the primary colours of paints, which are red, yellow and blue.

MIXING COLOURED LIGHT

There are two types of cell in the eye. Rod-shaped cells enable us to see in the dark. These cells cannot detect colour, which explains why only shades of grey can be seen after dark. Cone-shaped cells enable us to see colour. Some of these cone cells are sensitive to red light, some to green light, and some to blue light. As yellow is between red and green on the spectrum it has an equal effect on both the red and green cells. The brain recognizes this effect as yellow (Figure 5.12).

The children can try mixing the primary colours of light. Three strong torches should be covered with red-, blue- and green-coloured filters and shone on to a white toy or piece of paper to see how the various colours combine. Green and blue light combine

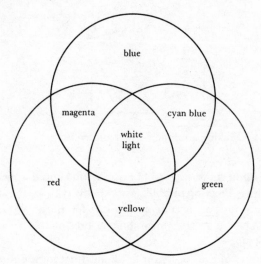

Figure 5.12 The primary colours of light

to make cyan blue; blue and red light make magenta; and green and red light make yellow. Together all three should give white light, but only if the colours are pure and projected at the same intensity. It is not necessary to add all the colours of the spectrum to get white light. Commercially produced filters are needed as cellophane contains impurities but the latter is very useful for models.

Model tetrahedra made out of different-coloured cellophanes are an attractive way of using the effect of mixing coloured light. Each child needs a piece of card about 40 cm by 40 cm. A set of four small equilateral triangles should be drawn with a 1 cm border on the card, as shown in Figure 5.13.

The children can glue differently coloured cellophane to fit each window. Once the model has dried it can be folded up to make a tetrahedron, with the edges fixed by sticky tape. The children could twist the model to look at the effect of the combination of colours and note what they see.

Making coloured glasses is an enjoyable way to see the effect of different coloured filters. The children can cut out some cardboard glasses and put red cellophane in one pair of glasses and green in another pair. They can investigate what happens when they look through the glasses at pictures using only green crayons and others

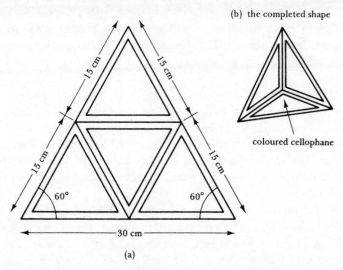

(b) the completed shape

coloured cellophane

15 cm 15 cm 15 cm 15 cm 60° 60° 30 cm

(a)

Figure 5.13 Coloured tetrahedron

using only red crayons. When the children look through the green cellophane all colours except green are filtered out so that the red drawing will appear to be black. Only the cells sensitive to green can respond and there is no green in the drawing.

If the children crayon or paint the colours of the rainbow onto a circular disc and spin it at high speed the eye will appear to see the colours as one. As the colouring cannot be completely accurate the colours will seem to blend into cream rather than white.

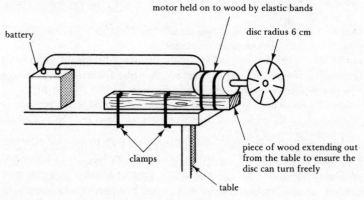

motor held on to wood by elastic bands

battery

disc radius 6 cm

clamps

piece of wood extending out from the table to ensure the disc can turn freely

table

Figure 5.14 Spinning coloured discs

The children can then try several discs with different patterns and combinations of colours. They should predict what might happen before testing. If the children set up the equipment for themselves it will give them an opportunity to apply electrical skills as well.

Coloured paints have a different set of primary colours because the paints act like filters by removing some of the light falling on them. For example, yellow paint removes all light except red, yellow and green. Cyan paint removes all light except blue and green. Therefore, when cyan and yellow are mixed, the only colour the paint does not absorb is green, i.e. cyan blue and yellow paint make green.

As the physics of colour is not simple, children in the primary school should be mainly encouraged to investigate mixing different coloured light and to report their observations. In the secondary school they will be able to refer back to this practical experience to enhance their understanding. The explanations are added here to attempt to clarify the difference between the primary colours of paint and light for teachers.

FURTHER READING

Balding, G. and Richards, N. (1980) *Springboards: Ideas for Science*. Melbourne: Thomas Nelson.

Coldrey, J. and Goldie-Morrison, K. (eds) (1986) *Danger Colours*. London: André Deutsch.

Coldrey, J. and Goldie-Morrison, K. (eds) (1986) *Hide and Seek*. London: André Deutsch.

Department of Education and Science and the Welsh Office (1989) *Science in the National Curriculum*. London: HMSO.

Diamond, D. (1976) *Mirrors and Magnifiers*. London: Macdonald Educational.

Driver, R., Guesne, E. and Tiberghien, A. (eds) (1985) *Children's Ideas in Science*. Milton Keynes: Open University Press.

Gilbert, C. and Matthews, P. (1981) *Look*. London: Addison-Wesley.

Jennings, T. (1982) *The Young Scientist Investigates: Light and Colour*. Oxford: Oxford University Press.

Jennings, T. (1989) *Into Science: Colour*. Oxford: Oxford University Press.

Kinçaid, D., Rapson, H. and Richards, R. (1983) *Science for Children with Learning Difficulties*. London: Macdonald Educational/Schools Council.

Kincaid, D. and Richards, R. (1981) *Colour*. London: Macdonald/Schools Council Publications.

Parker, S. (1973) *Science 5/13: Coloured Things Stages 1 and 2*. London: Macdonald/Schools Council.

Parker, S. (1985) *Step into Science: Light*. London: Granada.

Richards, J. (1981) *Light and Colour*. London: Macmillan Education/West Sussex C.C.

Showell, R. (1979) *Teaching Science to Infants*. London: Ward Lock Educational.

Walpole, B. (1987) *Fun with Science: Light*. London: Kingfisher Books.

Walter, M. (1971) *Make a Bigger Puddle, Make a Smaller Worm*. London: André Deutsch.

Watson, P. (1982) *Science Club: Light Fantastic*. London: Methuen.

CHAPTER 6

Magnetism and Electricity

KEY STAGES 1 AND 2
Investigations into magnetism should start in the early years. These experiences can then be reinforced and established in junior classes by developing the links between magnetism and electricity and by giving children opportunities to use their expertise in open-ended scientific and technology problems.

Young children need the opportunity to play with devices that use batteries, wires and bulbs, perhaps as part of investigations into toys. Detailed investigations into different types of circuits, experiments to find insulators and conductors, and switching systems are more appropriate for the early junior years. Older juniors are required to have had more advanced experiences of varying electrical flows and the heating and magnetic effects of electricity, but they are not assessed on it. An appreciation of the dangers of electricity is important from the very early years and should be continually reinforced.

Magnetism

EXPLORING THE MAGNET AND MAGNETISM

Ideally, children should have the opportunity to play with toys that contain magnets so that their curiosity is aroused from an early age. When the children start to investigate magnetism they need to be provided with a wide variety of strengths and shapes of magnets so that they do not think that all magnets must be a particular shape or colour. Initially, the children can be given a variety of small objects including pins, nails, paper-clips, rubbers, keys, coins, candles, foil, glass, wood, paper and plastic and asked to find out what the magnet does. They should try to observe carefully and report anything they find interesting, including the shape and feel of the magnet as well as what effect it has. They might notice that only some objects are picked up; objects move towards the magnet before it touches them; several objects can appear to stick together to form a chain attached to the magnet; and only part of an object might be attracted. This type of open-ended investigation enables the teacher and children to raise questions or ideas to investigate further.

Once the children have discovered that not all materials are attracted to magnets they can investigate what is special about the 'magnetic set'. If they separate a set of magnetic objects from a set of non-magnetic objects they may be able to suggest what is the characteristic of each set. Once having made a suggestion, they can test their hypothesis by predicting which new objects should belong to each set and then testing their prediction. They may say all spoons are magnetic. In which case, if they test a new set of spoons which includes plastic and wooden ones, they should find that this generalization is incorrect and a new suggestion is needed. It is quite possible for young children to carry out this basic scientific procedure with the guidance of their teacher. The children should discover that the magnet only picks up metal objects. However, not all metals are magnetic. At this point the teacher will probably have to explain that there are different metals and provide examples of them for the children to test. It is possible that the children may know that differences in metals are significant if they have noticed that cans for re-cycling are sorted by using magnets.

In order to investigate magnets further the children can be set a number of simple problems:

- How many paper-clips can a bar magnet pick up if it is dropped into a pile of paper-clips? Is the answer about the same each time the activity is repeated? Can they find a way of recording the results?
- When a bar magnet is dropped into a pile of paper-clips, where on the magnet do the clips stay? Where is the strongest part of the magnet? Can paper-clips be suspended from the middle or only the ends? Do the two ends pick up the same number of clips?
- How many paper-clips can be suspended in one line when they are linked together? Is it the same, less, or more than if a line of clips are touching but not linked?

- What is the maximum number of paper-clips that can be suspended on one magnet?
- How far away can a magnet be held and still be able to pick up a paper-clip? Do bigger or heavier magnets have more strength? Can the children find a way of testing magnets? One way is to suspend a screw or nail on a string above the zero point on a ruler. The magnet to be tested is slowly moved along from the far end of the ruler. The point where the nail is pulled towards the magnet is recorded. Stronger magnets will exert a pull from a longer distance.
- Can a magnet's power work through other materials? Will the paper-clip still be picked up if the magnet is held on the other side of a sheet of paper, metal, glass or plastic; or through water? The children should discover that a magnetic field passes through non-magnetic material.

The pull or force of magnetism through non-magnetic materials can be used and illustrated by making simple toys. The children can make a small boat out of card or cork with a screw fixed to the bottom. The boat is floated in a shallow container and moved around by moving a magnet underneath the container. A race track or street might be prepared on a sheet of card and then matchbox cars, with paper-clips or nails inside, are moved about by using magnets underneath.

Although it is important to set specific problems or questions to help focus the children's discoveries, the children also need periods of free 'play' or exploration with the equipment to enable them to repeat and check previous activities and to raise and investigate their own ideas.

USING MAGNETS FOR SORTING

It is important that children start to recognize the applications of the different properties of materials so that they can appreciate the significance of science in their lives. As magnets mainly attract objects made of iron, steel (which contains iron), nickel and cobalt, they can be used to sort out these metals for removal or use. The children can carry out a simple activity to demonstrate the use of magnets for cleaning. If they file rust from an old can and mix the filings well into sugar a magnet can then be used to retrieve the rust particles. Similarly, lost ball-bearings can be regained from a sand tray. The children might use books to find other examples of using magnets for sorting: e.g. as metal detectors, for cleaning oil, and to collect iron for re-smelting.

USING MAGNETS FOR HOLDING AND LIFTING

The children could look for situations where magnets are used in their own environment. Magnets are quite often used to hold things up (notice holders); to ensure a door closes properly (fridge doors); to lift things (cat flaps); and on cranes to lift iron-based objects without having to hook or clamp them. The children could make a working model crane using a magnet (details are given later in this chapter). As part of the design stage of the model they might investigate how much weight different magnets can lift. A yoghurt pot on a string attached to a safety pin or paper-clip could be weighted with 1-gram weights to see what weight different magnets can lift.

A fishing game using magnets is easy for young children to make. The children cut out fish shapes from card or plastic. A paper-clip is fixed to each fish. The children then catch the fish using a fishing rod made with string and a magnet on the end as the hook. If the fish are numbered, the children can total the numbers on their catch and the child with the highest score wins.

MAGNETS CAN MAKE OTHER MAGNETS

During play the children may have noticed that the paper-clips they have been using have become magnetic. The ions (charged particles) in a magnet are all aligned between the north and south poles. Other pieces of iron and steel can become magnetic if their particles are also aligned in this way. A pin, nail or needle can be magnetized by stroking it with a magnet about 20 times. It is essential to use the same end of the magnet and to stroke the nail in the same direction every time.

If the new magnet is knocked or dropped the particles will lose their alignment. The children could discover how many knocks are necessary. This will also happen with bought magnets, which is why they must be carefully stored, with like poles together and positioned so they cannot be knocked.

INVESTIGATING MAGNETIC POLES

In order to discover that each magnet has a north and south pole the children should mark one end of a bar magnet with a coloured dot of paper. They should then suspend the magnet above the floor on a piece of string and allow it to settle. A paper arrow on the floor showing the way the magnet is pointing will record its direction. If the exercise is repeated, the children should discover that the magnet always points the same way. It is important that each magnet is kept away from other magnets or metal objects as these will affect the results.

It is this consistent directional property of magnets that enables them to be used as compasses. When a magnet is suspended or resting on something that floats, so that it can turn freely, one end will always point north and one end will point south. The ends of the magnet are referred to as either the north pole or south pole as appropriate. Initially, the only way to find out which is which is to use a compass. The children will probably have some understanding of the points of a compass from watching the television, and Muslims use a compass regularly to ascertain the direction of Mecca for prayer. Once the north and south poles have been marked on the magnets by using a compass, the magnets themselves can be used as compasses.

A needle can be magnetized in order to make a compass. The magnetized needle should be fixed on a card with the compass directions marked. This is then glued onto a cork. If the cork is floated on water, it will turn easily and settle pointing north. The children will discover that if they move a magnet near a compass, it will disturb the needle because it is made of magnetic material. Consequently, a compass should always be read away from metal objects. Rocks containing iron can cause havoc to explorers.

When the children play with the magnets they will probably discover that two magnets sometimes pull towards each other and sometimes they repel each other. Once the magnets have the north and south poles marked, the children can try and work out why this occurs. If two magnets, still suspended from strings, are brought close together, the children should discover that two north poles will attract, as will two south poles, but a north and south repel. The force involved is quite strong, even in the small magnets usually available in schools. The children can experience this by lightly holding a magnet and trying to force two unlike poles together. If ring magnets are available, place them over a vertical rod with unlike poles adjacent. The magnets will appear to be suspended in the air with nothing to hold them up. It is actually the force of the two poles repelling each other that keeps them apart. The children may like to make a set of train carriages from small boxes with magnets used as coupling devices. Using the north and south poles of magnets will ensure that only the fronts and backs of trucks can be joined, even if the magnets cannot be seen. On the other hand, if opposite poles are placed facing each other, as one truck is moved, a second will be pushed along without the trucks touching.

The pattern of the magnetic field of one or two magnets can be seen by using iron filings. If the filings are placed on a piece of paper and the magnet is placed underneath, a two-dimensional pattern is seen. This pattern can be kept permanently by spraying it with lacquer. If the filings are put into a transparent plastic box and one or two magnets placed on the box, a three-dimensional pattern will be seen. This has the advantage that the fillings do not get spread everywhere and lost.

Electricity

Although electricity is in a separate category in the National Curriculum it overlaps into many other areas. Electricity is an important energy source and pupils are expected to develop knowledge and understanding of the nature of energy, its transfer and control. The control of electricity by switching systems is an essential part of transfer of information in telephones and computers. Batteries are frequently used in models for technology projects.

As a general safety measure children must always be warned not to play with mains electricity. If the children have the opportunity to play with and investigate toys with batteries as part of studies on forces and energy, this important rule should be emphasized. Work on care of ourselves and our environment can include safety in the home and around the school. When older children are investigating circuits and batteries, and considering electricity as an energy source, the dangers of mains electricity must again be stressed.

The electricity boards can provide very good material to provoke discussions with children about using electricity safely in the home, the dangers of flying kites or fishing near overhead wires and the importance of keeping away from substations. To encourage the children to think about safety aspects and how to apply appropriate safety measures they could be asked to design a poster giving advice or a warning about electricity. As the actual wording and its presentation is an essential part of an effective poster, aspects of language and art work can also be developed alongside the science work.

Most of the basic work on circuits is likely to be most appropriate in the early junior years. The children's knowledge can then be extended through the media of other science topics and technology activities. It is important to link work with batteries to real situations so that a topic on electricity has relevance, while at the same time making the children aware of the dangers of mains electricity.

MAKING SIMPLE CIRCUITS

There are a number of terms that could be used in electrical work with children, such as current and voltage, which they find difficult to understand. Children at key stages 1 and 2 are not required to use these terms. The term 'electrical energy' is preferable to 'current'. Children will have already used the term 'energy' and have some idea of its meaning. It is easy for children to misuse the word current since, unlike electrical energy, it cannot be used up. Therefore it is incorrect to say that the current is being expended when a bulb is on. Current is rather like the water in a central heating system, which is not consumed but is the means to convey heat energy. A foundation given at this stage based on using the term electrical energy will enable the children to have a good grasp of these more complicated concepts at a later date.

Junior children do need to establish the concepts relating to a circuit. They find it difficult to think of the battery having a difference between the terminals which causes the flow to balance the differentials, particularly if the battery has only one obvious terminal. Instead they often think of the battery as a source of energy and the lamp as the consumer, so that electrical energy flows from the battery to the lamp and the second wire in the return path is not needed. The children may suggest the second wire is a safety wire or like a catalyst, just there to get the bulb to light. Consequently it is advisable to use batteries with two pronounced terminals. The teacher will need to explain to the children that the bulb lights up because the electrical energy moving through it makes the thin wire become very hot and glow.

A good start to investigations about electricity is to provide a battery, bulb and two bare wires and to ask the children to find a way of lighting the bulb. They will only succeed if one wire travels from the terminal to the side of the bulb and the other wire goes from the base of the bulb to the second terminal (Figure 6.1a). Once they have succeeded they can be given a bulb-holder and asked to repeat the activity with the bulb in the holder (Figure 6.1b). It is a good idea for the teacher to practise putting bulb-holders back together beforehand as sometimes the holders are dismantled by the children in an attempt to solve the problem.

Worksheets setting out simple problems help the children to discover the factors necessary to light a bulb (Figure 6.2). If the children try to predict what will happen before they set up the circuit they are more likely to think carefully about their observations. A complete circuit from one terminal to another is necessary. The electricity will also take the shortest and easiest route and

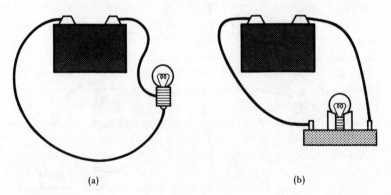

(a)   (b)

Figure 6.1 Lighting a bulb

Will the bulb light or not? Tell your partner what you think will happen and why *before* you try it. When you have tried all the examples make a list of what factors are necessary to light a bulb.

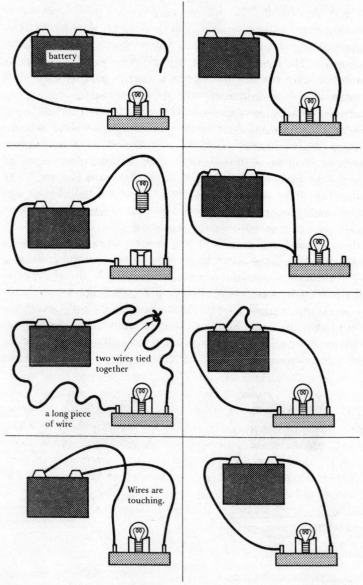

Figure 6.2 Making a bulb light

so may bypass the bulb. This will happen if the wires touch, causing a short, or if one circuit is much shorter than the others.

TWO OR MORE BULBS IN A CIRCUIT

When the children are able to make a circuit with one bulb they can try to light two or three. Again, different tasks can be provided to enable the children to realize that the more bulbs there are in series, i.e. one after the other on a wire, the dimmer each bulb becomes. Two or more bulbs offer more resistance in the circuit and therefore the light is dimmer. If the bulbs are in parallel, each circuit is separate and therefore the bulbs remain bright, but the battery is used up more rapidly (Figures 6.3 and 6.4). The children might consider the advantages and disadvantages of each type of wiring, and which is more appropriate for wiring a house. If houses were not wired in parallel, when one bulb blew all the lights would go out. As part of the activity the class could compare how long a battery lasts for each type of circuit.

It is important that the children realize that batteries have a limited life so that they start to appreciate that most energy sources are unrenewable and need to be used carefully. This may reduce the risk of all the school's batteries being run down by children who are reluctant to dismantle their experiments at the end of a session.

When buying bulbs and batteries for school use it is important to get compatible ones. Some batteries are too strong for the bulbs and they are quickly blown. On the other hand, some batteries are too weak to light certain bulbs. If possible, a variety of shapes of batteries should be provided so that the children are aware of the differences. The children might investigate different batteries. What different voltages do they have? Do they light a bulb to the same brightness? Do two batteries make a bulb burn more brightly? Does it make any difference how two batteries are joined together? Children could look at the similarities and differences of a variety of bulbs in the same way. A careful study of the bulbs should enable the children to notice the filament in the bulb which gets white-hot to give off light.

INSULATORS AND CONDUCTORS

To enable the children to discover that not all materials conduct electricity they need to make a simple circuit to light a bulb as

Make these circuits. Look carefully at the brightness of the bulb.

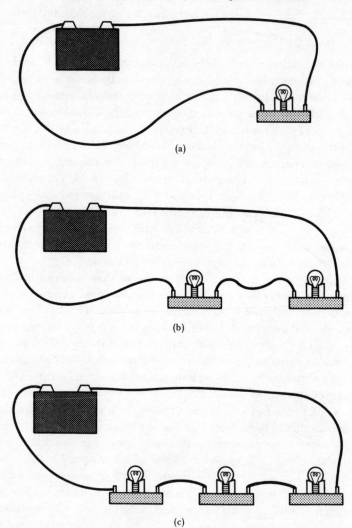

(a)

(b)

(c)

1. If there are two bulbs in a circuit, is each bulb as bright as the one on its own?

2. What happens to the brightness when there are three bulbs?

3. What do you think will happen if there are four bulbs? Try it.

Figure 6.3 Sample worksheet: lighting more than one bulb

Try these ways of lighting two bulbs.

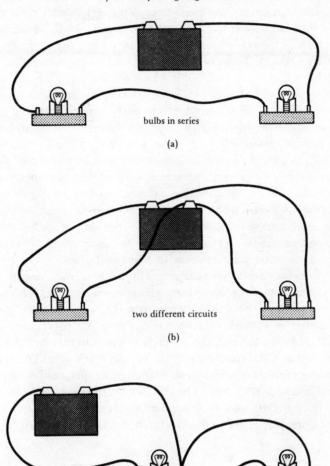

(a)

bulbs in series

(b)

two different circuits

(c)

bulbs in parallel

1. Are some bulbs brighter than others?

2. What happens in each circuit if one bulb is taken out or breaks?

3. Which way of joining the bulbs is best for household lights? Why?

4. Can you light four bulbs?

Figure 6.4 Sample worksheet: finding the best way to light two or three bulbs

before but to replace one of the connecting wires with different materials. They could try a variety of items such as string, plastic, aluminium foil, coat-hangers, rubber bands, wool, wood and glass. The children should discover that only metal conducts electricity. Using this information, they can try to invent a way of covering a bare wire so that it does not cause a short if it touches another bare wire. Usually children are very imaginative and use a wide variety of items ranging from pasta, straws, fabric, paper and wool to sticky tape. The children could then examine insulated wire flex and learn how to prepare it for use.

Children need to know that water is a good conductor of electricity so that they can appreciate why they should not have electrical equipment in a steamy bathroom or touch a switch with wet hands. A circuit with a battery and bulb can be set up as shown in Figure 6.5 to demonstrate this. This idea can be applied for a flood alarm. As the water level rises, the ends of the wires are covered and electricity can flow to a buzzer or bell.

Some metals are better conductors than others, e.g. copper and brass. But even these have their effectiveness reduced by being rusty or greasy. This can be demonstrated by giving the children a prepared set of nails which are rusty, painted, dirty, greasy or left clean. When the children try these in their circuits they should discover that metal conducts best if it is clean and bright. The other substances either act as insulators or change the surface of the metal so that it is no longer pure. The children should now have enough knowledge to find out why an appliance does not work. They could either dismantle or try to mend a torch that is no longer working.

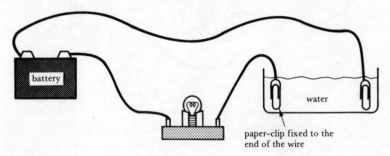

Figure 6.5 Circuit to demonstrate that water is a good conductor of electricity

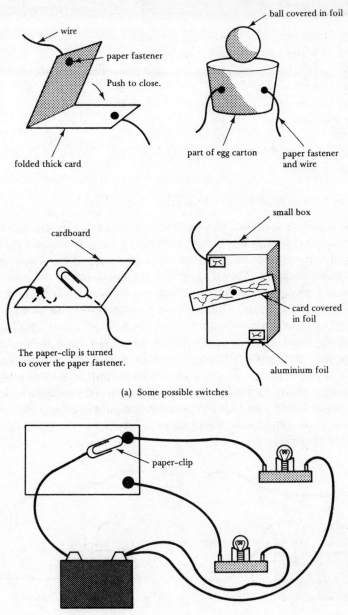

(a) Some possible switches

(b) A two-way switch

Figure 6.6 Switches

105

SWITCHES

The simplest way of controlling electricity is by an on/off switch. The children can be asked to try to invent a way of controlling a break in the wire using paper-clips, drawing pins, metal foil, coins, wire, cardboard and balsa wood (Figure 6.6a). They could also find out the effect of placing the switch in different places in a circuit. Once the children can place a switch in one circuit the teacher might suggest that they invent a two-way switch to light either a red bulb or a green bulb. One possible solution is shown in Figure 6.6b.

VARYING THE FLOWS OF ELECTRICITY

Some metals conduct electricity much better than others. A dimmer switch uses this property. Some of the children may have a dimmer switch in their bedrooms if they prefer not to sleep in complete darkness. They may be able to suggest other places where they are used, e.g. in a theatre or hospital ward. To make a dimmer switch, set up a zigzag board using nichrome wire, as shown in Figure 6.7. When drawing pin 1 is touched, the circuit is complete and the bulb lights brightly. When drawing pins 2 to 10 are touched, the electricity has to flow through more nichrome wire. This type of wire is resistant to the electric current. The more there is in the circuit, the dimmer the light becomes. If the children make a similar board with ordinary wire for comparison, they will find there is no appreciable dimming of the bulb as this wire offers minimal resistance.

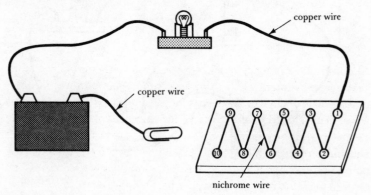

Figure 6.7 A dimmer switch

MAKING MODELS USING ELECTRICAL CIRCUITS

By eight or nine years old the children should have enough experience of making electrical circuits and switches to apply their knowledge. Groups of children can make different models of varying complexity depending on their ability. Ideally the children should be given minimal information as to how to make the model. The design, material to be used, method of construction and circuit are all parts of the problem to be solved:

- A flashing lighthouse.
- A torch with switch.
- A dolls' house with one bulb or with several in series. Ambitious children might have a television or cooker that lights up.
- A model mosque, gurdwara or church with coloured tissue-paper windows.
- A theatre with footlights and perhaps a dimmer switch.
- A car with red lights at the back and white lights at the front.
- A monster with flashing eyes.
- A steady hand tester with a bell or buzzer.
- A quiz board that lights up or rings a bell if the answer is correct.
- Traffic lights that show the sequence red, red and amber, green, then amber.
- A morse code transmitter using either a buzzer or light.
- An alarm switch that detects the arrival of a visitor, or protects a precious object from a thief.
- A flood warning system.

USING ELECTRICITY

Electricity is an energy source that is used to create light, sound, heat and movement. The children could collect pictures of different electrical devices from catalogues and set them in various ways. The children will already have had experience of using electricity for producing light and sound by using bulbs, bells and buzzers in their circuits. They may also have noticed that bulbs become hot when lit. To understand how electricity can be used to create movement, upper junior children need to explore electromagnetism.

A steady hand tester

stiff wire
(An old coat
hanger will do.)

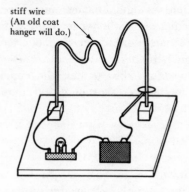

Traffic lights

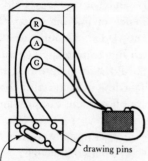

drawing pins

A paper-clip is moved to change
the lights. If the red and amber
drawing pins are close, both lights
will light together.

Quiz board

paper fastener

cardboard

insulated wire
underneath to
link correct
answers

horse ○ ○ calf
cat ○ ○ foal
cow ○ ○ puppy
dog ○ ○ kitten

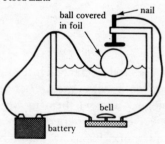

Morse code transmitter

A thin piece of metal
is pushed down to
complete the circuit.

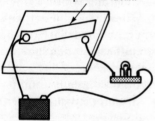

Flood alarm

ball covered
in foil

nail

bell

battery

As the ball covered in foil rises with the
water it touches the nail and completes
the circuit. The bell rings.

Door alarm (for an escaping hamster)

Thick card. When it is stepped on it is
flattened and then completes the circuit.

cage door

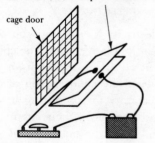

Figure 6.8 Electrical circuit models

108

USING ELECTRICITY TO MAKE A MAGNET

A magnet can only be made out of magnetic material, i.e. iron, steel, cobalt and nickel. The children should wrap covered wire around an iron nail about 20 times. It does not matter if the turns of the wire overlap (Figure 6.9a). When the wires are connected to a battery the nail will act as a magnet. The children can test the effect of different numbers of turns around the nail. They can find out how many paper-clips the nail will pick up with 10, 20, 50, or more turns. The children could investigate what happens if two batteries joined together are used; what happens when the electric current is turned off; or whether other types of metal or other materials work as electromagnets.

The children could make a crane which uses an electromagnet (Figure 6.9b). When the current is switched on it lifts steel or iron and drops it when the current is switched off. Electromagnets are used to move steel and iron scrap at steel furnaces because they also have the effect of preventing other metals and non-metallic rubbish getting into the steel furnaces.

These types of activities cause batteries to run down quite quickly. The children need to be aware that this may influence their results and know to be careful in the use of their batteries. For this reason some of the activities may need to be in fairly large supervised groups.

From previous activities the children will probably have found out that magnets make a compass go awry. The magnetic effect of electricity has the same effect. This can be shown if the children

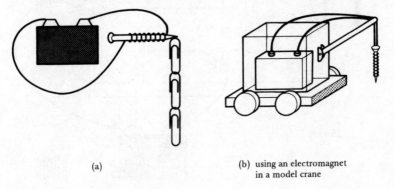

(a)

(b) using an electromagnet in a model crane

Figure 6.9 Making electromagnets

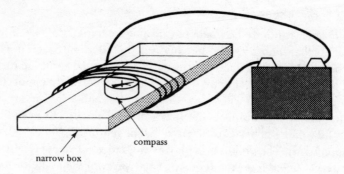

narrow box

compass

Figure 6.10 Magnetic effect of electricity on a compass

wind wire around a narrow box about six times and then put a compass inside the box so that the compass needle is parallel to the wire (Figure 6.10). When the ends of the wire are connected to the battery, the needle will move to one side. They could investigate further by reporting what happens when the wires are changed round to the opposite terminals; and what happens when there are 12 coils around the box. They should discover that the greater the number of turns the greater is the deflection of the needle.

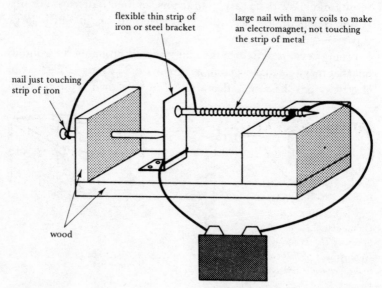

flexible thin strip of iron or steel bracket

large nail with many coils to make an electromagnet, not touching the strip of metal

nail just touching strip of iron

wood

Figure 6.11 How electricity is used to create movement and sound

110

An electromagnet can be used to make a buzzer which will demonstrate how electricity is used to create movement and sound. When the current is on, the metal strip is pulled towards the electromagnet. This breaks the circuit so the strip jumps back to complete the circuit again. This is repeated rapidly to give a buzzing noise (Figure 6.11).

DRAWING AND RECORDING CIRCUITS

Initially, when the children record their findings or prepare a design for a model or experiment they could use their own way of representing the various parts of the circuit. Subsequently the different symbols could be discussed and compared with codes or symbols on a map or weather chart. A good symbol should give a clue to the original object; it should be easily and quickly reproduced; not be easily confused with other symbols; and in the case of electricity be capable of being joined with other symbols to represent a variety of circuits. The accepted codes in general use are as shown in Figure 6.12.

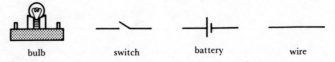

bulb   switch   battery   wire

Figure 6.12 Accepted codes in use

FURTHER READING

Amery, H. and Littler, A. (1975) *The Knowhow Book of Batteries and Magnets*. London: Usborne.

Ardley, N. (1986) *Exploring Magnetism*. London: Franklin Watts.

Brown, B. (1989) *Electricity for Life: 2. In the Environment*. Hobsons Publishing/ The Electricity Board.

Clements, P. and Livingstone, S. (1988) *Electricity for Life: 1. At Home and around Us*. Hobsons Publishing/The Electricity Board.

Department of Education and Science and the Welsh Office (1989) *Science in the National Curriculum*. London: HMSO.

Driver, R., Guesne, E. and Tiberghien, A. (eds) (1985) *Children's Ideas in Science*. Milton Keynes: Open University Press.

Kincaid, D., Rapson, H. and Richards, R. (1983) *Science for Children with Learning Difficulties*. London: Macdonald Educational.

Radford, D. (1972) *Science from Toys*. London: Macdonald Educational/ Schools Council.

Reid, K. (1989) *Electricity for Life: 3. Communication*. Hobsons Publishing/The Electricity Board.

CHAPTER 7
Sound and Music

The National Curriculum requires that during the early years children should explore sounds in their own environment to find out about their causes and uses. They should investigate ways of sorting these sounds and those produced by musical instruments. Simple musical instruments, from different cultural traditions, should be studied and made with a view to helping the children to understand that sound can be produced in a variety of ways.

Investigation activities in key stage 2 should extend this foundation to help children to understand that sounds are produced by vibrating objects, can be changed by changing the material, size and tension, and can travel through different media. In the later years the children should also consider the effect of sounds and noise on the quality of the environment.

EARLY YEARS

Sounds in the environment

Although children are aware of many sounds in the environment they rarely listen carefully in order to distinguish and describe them. Several activities can heighten the awareness of different sounds in an enjoyable way. The children will probably be surprised at the number of things they can hear if they try to keep absolutely quiet for two or three minutes: pencils moving on paper, breathing, heartbeats, the class pet moving, coughing, etc. From this start they could write a story or poem, draw pictures or make a list of sounds that might be heard in the school from early in the morning when the caretaker arrives through the day, including typical noises heard when the children arrive, in the classrooms, playground, dining-room and hall.

Further activities to encourage children to describe sounds and try to guess their origin might include guessing games in which one child drops or moves an object behind a screen for the others to identify; trying to guess the identity of hidden objects in containers; or guessing what is happening on prepared tape recordings of common household tasks. Once the children have begun to distinguish and describe sounds, they could go on a listening walk around the school and its environs, where they might hear traffic, machines, birds, footsteps, the action of the wind and so on. A group could prepare their own recording of typical sounds in the neighbourhood.

The sounds can be sorted in a variety of ways. The children may suggest that they identify pleasant or unpleasant, loud or soft, and high or low sounds. A set of warning sounds could include fire alarms, ambulance, fire engine and police sirens, babies crying or screaming, and animal warning noises such as rabbits thumping their back legs and a gerbil's high-pitched cry. A discussion about the children's pets will help the children realize that animals not only make warning noises but also use sound to denote pleasure, ask for food, warn off enemies and attract mates.

Humans make a great variety of sounds. The children can try to make different sounds with different parts of their bodies such as clapping, clicking fingers, rubbing hands, tapping a leg or stamping feet. Most human sounds, however, are made with the voice to speak, laugh, cry or sing. If the children put their hands gently on the front of their throats while they are singing or talking they will feel the voice box vibrating. During breathing in, the vocal cords are pulled apart, but when we speak they are brought close together so that they partially block the air being breathed out. A similar action can be demonstrated by making a sound with air escaping from a blown-up balloon as the neck of the balloon is stretched sideways. The children should also notice that the tongue moves as well to make the variation in sound. If there are children who speak different languages in the class they can try to compare and contrast the different types of sound produced by each.

Examining musical instruments

Trying to describe and classify a collection of different musical instruments can start the children thinking about the way sounds are made. Ideally the collection should include instruments common to different cultures as well as those that are usually available in schools. Initially, each child could try to find a different way of playing one instrument. A tambourine could be shaken at different rates, the wood, metal or skin could be tapped or rubbed in different ways, and blowing will also produce a sound. As the children attempt to explain how the noises are produced they are likely to identify the main ways of playing instruments, i.e. by rubbing, plucking, blowing, tapping or shaking.

Making sounds to accompany stories also helps the children to think of different ways of making sounds. The teacher could tell a story and ask the children to suggest how they could make appropriate sounds from a collection of junk materials. From these experiences the children could make their own instrument out of junk materials or the teacher may decide to provide a more structured activity so that different groups make different types of instruments which can then be used to accompany the children's own stories (Figure 7.1).

KEY STAGE 2

Much of the work on sounds in the early years and junior classes can be incorporated into the school music and singing activities. To understand the science concepts it is important that the children can distinguish between loud and soft, and high and low sounds. This skill is probably best developed over time as part of general music activities.

Sounds and vibrations

Sound is made when something vibrates. When a drum is tapped the children can feel the skin vibrating. Putting a finger on the top will stop or dampen the vibrations, showing the link between sound and vibration. If the children hold a ruler on a table so that it extends over the edge and bend and release the free end it too will vibrate and make a noise. Similarly, when a taut rubber band is plucked it vibrates quickly to produce a sound. When the

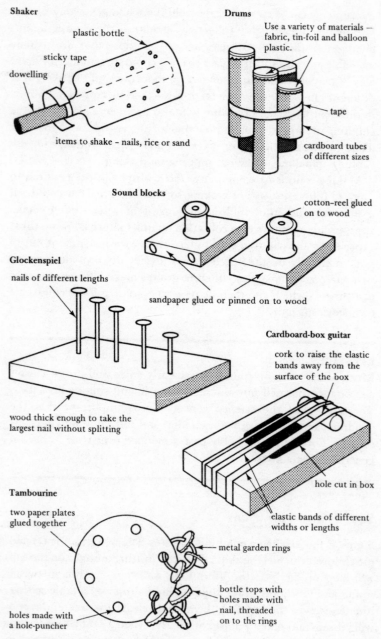

Figure 7.1 Making instruments

116

vibrations are fast a high sound is produced and when they are slow low sounds are created. Humans cannot hear all sounds. The children may already know about dog whistles which appear to make no sound but dogs hear and respond to them.

Without vibrations a sound cannot be produced. When a bicycle bell is rung the children can see that the hammer makes the cover vibrate. If the cover is held, stopping the vibrations, the sound is reduced. As the bell rings, it causes the air around it to vibrate and sound waves move outwards. The further the sound waves travel the weaker they become; therefore, a distant sound is not heard as clearly as a close one. Although the children cannot see sound waves moving through the air they can see the same action when a marble or droplet of water is dropped into a pond or large container of water. The circular ripples move outwards from the splash in the same way as sound waves. If a large stone is dropped into the water, the splash is louder and the waves are larger and move out further.

By watching the ripples closely the children may be able to see that the waves vary in speed, height and closeness. Sound waves also vary in their size. When children blow up a balloon they can appreciate that air has substance and is springy. If they hold the balloon to their ear and tap it they will hear a sound. Each tap presses the outside of the balloon and squashes the air particles, making a wave in the air in the same way as a tap on the surface of the water makes a wave.

A skipping rope may help children to understand how waves can move along a substance without it actually moving forward. Two children hold the rope taut and then make a wave at one end by shaking it. The children should see the movement of the wave as it travels down the length of the rope. They can try to work out how to make small and large waves. They should find that agitating a long piece of rope will produce long waves and a short piece will produce short waves.

Sound waves that are short obviously produce more vibrations per second. Short sound waves produce a higher note than long ones, and are generated in short, thin and taut materials. This relationship can be found in different materials and musical instruments. The thin, short and taut strings on a guitar produce high notes, as do short, narrow columns of air in a wind instrument and thin, taut and small drum skins. Several activities can be provided to enable children to discover these relationships for themselves.

Sounds and length

The relationship between length and difference of pitch can be investigated by experimenting with a set of wooden rods made from dowelling cut to different lengths. If each rod has a string loop with a peg at one end, the children can easily move them about on a line. The rods can then be ranked so that the ones producing the highest sounds are at one end and those producing the lowest sounds at the other (Figure 7.2).

Rods made of metal piping will produce a different sound but also show that the longest pieces make the lowest sounds. If the children made a glockenspiel (Figure 7.1), they will have found the longest nails again make the lowest sounds. To assess whether the children can transfer this knowledge the teacher could ask the children to fix a ruler to the edge of a desk with a clamp and predict the different sounds that will be produced when the length of the ruler extending beyond the edge of the desk is varied. The children can then carry out the activity to test their predictions.

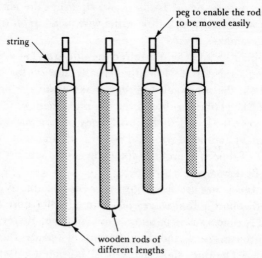

Figure 7.2 Investigating the relationship between length and sound

Sound and thickness

Different pairs of dowelling of the same length but different thicknesses can be tested to ascertain whether thickness of material has any effect on sound. Each pair should be tapped and ordered according to the pitch produced. Similarly, nails of the same length but with different thicknesses can be hammered into a block of wood in order of pitch. The children should find out that the thicker rods and nails produce the lowest notes. In the same way a thick string on a piano or guitar makes a lower note than a thin string of the same length because it is heavier and cannot vibrate so quickly.

The effect of combining thickness and length can be tested by using elastic bands. The children can put different bands round a cardboard box to compare the different sounds produced. Initially they must be careful to change one variable at a time. If they are comparing thickness, the length must remain the same. Later they can combine variables and compare the sounds produced by a long thick band, a long thin band, a short thick band and a short thin band. Following these activities the children may appreciate why lower sounding string instruments not only have longer strings but also thicker ones.

Sound and tension

Tension also affects the sound of stringed instruments. If an elastic band is placed over a hook or top of a chair and plucked when it is loose and then as it is steadily stretched, it will produce an increasingly higher note.

Distance and speed of sound

Children can experiment with the distance that sound will travel. Groups could be asked to design and carry out an investigation to discover how far the sound of a ticking clock will travel. They will probably listen at various distances moving away from the source of the sound to determine when they can no longer hear the sound. As they carry out the investigation the children will probably realize that some of their group hear the sound better than others.

This enables the teacher to discuss the importance of identifying all the variables that affect one observation. After discussion the children may be able to suggest some of the different factors that influence the distance the sound travels, such as the hearing of the testers; what the clock has been placed on; whether the clock has been muffled; whether there are any barriers between the sound and the listener and so on. The effect of these different factors could be tested by different children, each group making sure that only the variable they are testing is changed.

It is difficult to show children that sound takes time to travel as sounds appear instantaneous in the situations usually experienced by them. However, the idea can be considered during a thunderstorm. Although thunder is the sound made by the spark of electricity that produces the flash of lightning, it is often heard after the flash that made it has been seen because light travels faster than sound. The longer the gap between seeing the lightning and hearing the thunder the further away the storm is. As sound travels about 1 km in 3 seconds, if the children count the seconds after the flash, they can work out how far away the storm is.

Three conditions are necessary to hear sounds. Something is needed to make vibrations which then must travel through some type of substance and finally a receiver or ears must pick up and make sense of the vibrations.

Investigating which materials transmit sound

As sounds are transmitted by vibrations, they cannot be heard in a vacuum. Consequently messages in space must be transmitted by some other means, such as electrical or radio signals. Many children tend to assume that sound only travels through air whereas it is actually transmitted better in liquids and solids because the particles are closer together. Not so much energy is lost in the wave action when pushing close particles, so the sound is louder and reaches further.

Children can listen to sounds through different materials to decide for themselves whether sound can travel through different things. If they rest their ears on the desk and then tap the surface of the desk they should hear a louder sound than when they lift their head away from the desk. Pairs of children can experiment with water pipes or metal railings. One child should tap the metal with a stick while the other stands at a distance and compares the loudness of the sound produced with their ear against the railing or pipe compared to standing away from it. The children can discover that liquids transmit sound by tapping a piece of metal with a hammer under water while they listen with their ears against the water tank and apart.

A pair of telephones made from yoghurt cartons and a long piece of string also demonstrate that sounds travel better through solids than air. The string should be threaded through a hole made in the bottom of each pot and tied. One child walks away with one pot until the string is taut and holds the pot over their ear while their partner speaks into the other pot. The children should be able to hear each other fairly clearly. They can also experiment to find out what happens when the string is not tight, whether thick string is more effective than thin string and whether wire could be used instead of string. Compact hard string works well but not soft, whiskery types.

The effectiveness of different materials can be investigated by using a steady sound source such as a clock or battery-driven electric motor and rods or strips of wooden dowelling, metal, plastic, fabric, cotton wool and polystyrene. When the rods or strips about one metre long are placed on the sound source with the opposite end placed against, but not in, the ear, the children should find that the sounds produced by hard rigid substances are much louder.

Making sounds louder

Once a sound has been created it moves from its source in all directions. If it can be directed to move in one way, more of the sound energy will go in one direction. This is done when we cup our hands around the mouth. A simple megaphone made out of a piece of card rolled into a cone shape should demonstrate the same effect. A stethoscope is designed so that it collects as much as possible of the sound produced by the chest and directs it into the ear. A simple stethoscope can be made out of two plastic bottles and plastic tubing wide enough to fit over the bottle necks. The tops should be cut off each bottle to give a rounded end about 4 cm deep and fixed to the plastic tubes with sticky tape.

The difference between the loudness produced by solid and hollow materials can also be considered. Ideally the children should compare a solid block of wood with a hollow one of the same size and wood type. They can also compare two coffee jars, one full of water and the other empty; two boxes or tins, one full of sawdust or a cloth and the other empty. They should discover that hollow items produce a louder sound. The children can try placing the end of a tuning fork on to different sizes and shapes of cardboard boxes to see whether a large or small hollow produces a louder noise. This type of activity helps children to understand why a cello has a large wooden box but an electric guitar does not need one as it has electric amplifiers to increase the sound.

Catching sounds

The outer ear picks up the sound waves and leads them to the ear canal to make the eardrum and tiny bones inside the ear vibrate. This vibration stimulates nerves so that messages are sent and interpreted by the brain. Groups of children could devise their own test to discover who has the best hearing. They might then discuss how they could improve their hearing. Hopefully some will suggest that when they cup their hands and hold them by their ears they hear better as they are picking up more of the sound waves. Paper or cardboard ears could be made to fit over their ears and tested to see if they improve their hearing. The children would need to think of a fair way of testing the manufactured ears. They might suggest that they have a consistent sound and each child should walk towards it until it can be heard with and without the 'ears' and then collate the results.

Human and animal ears could be compared. The children could identify animals with prominent ears and then try to find out whether these use the sense of hearing as a major way of finding food or protecting themselves. This work might lead on to considering the value of two ears to ascertain the direction of sounds.

Controlling the sound in musical instruments

Musical instruments are designed to make specific sounds. Most have three main parts: something to make the vibration; something to amplify the sound; and a way to vary the note. As the children examine different instruments they can try to identify how each design meets these requirements.

A guitar has strings which are plucked to start the vibrations. The children should be able to see the movement by using a magnifying glass and notice that the string continues vibrating after the sound has died away. The different notes are produced by strings of different thicknesses and by shortening the strings as the fingers change position. If the children concentrate on one string and listen to the sound as the finger holding the string is moved from fret to fret they should hear the increasingly high note as the string is shortened. The sound is amplified by the bridge vibrating against the hollow wood. By lightly placing their fingers on the sound box as the guitar is played they should feel the vibrations.

Some instruments do not have strings but have pipes. In a simple instrument like a post-horn the movement of the lips creates the vibrations, the length of tubing and shape of the lips gives a particular note and the expanded end is designed to amplify the sound. When the instrument is blown the column of air vibrates. Pipes with different lengths and thicknesses have different sized columns of air. As with the long string or rod the longer the column of air the lower the note. The children can test the effect of varying the length of the column of air by using straws. About 1 cm at one end of a straw should be flattened and corners cut off to make a mouthpiece. With a bit of trial and error a sound can be produced by blowing through this mouthpiece. After predicting what will happen when the straw is shorter they should blow again and snip bits off the end of the straw as they blow. As the straw is shortened the note becomes higher.

Thick columns of air produce low notes in the same way as thick strings. When the children play a descant and bass recorder they will find that the latter has a lower note because it has a fatter, longer pipe. The holes along the top of the pipe enable the musician to vary the length of the air column. If fingers are placed over all of the holes the column will be long, producing a low note. As each finger is raised, the air column becomes shorter and the notes get higher. Other wind instruments have other ways of varying the length of the pipe. A trombone has an extendable pipe and a cornet uses valves.

Drums usually consist of a skin stretched tightly over a hollow frame. When the skin is hit, it and the air inside vibrate. If children make their own drums out of rubber stretched over tins or plastic boxes they can try to find out how to make drums with high and low notes. They should discover that the tighter the skin, the higher the note. Some African drums are played so that the tension of the skin is varied by pulling on the side strings. If the children have the opportunity to play or listen to drums of different sizes they may notice that the larger the skin the lower the note. As with the pipes a large volume of air inside the drum will also produce a low note. Consequently a wide deep drum with slightly slack skin will produce a low sound.

Whenever possible the children should predict what will happen before the investigations as this helps them to think about and clarify the concepts. As the ideas are likely to be very new to the children and involve using an unfamiliar vocabulary, they need plenty of time to play or explore the instruments for themselves to help them consolidate their ideas. Recapping work during later musical activities may enable children who have difficulties initially to recall and understand past experiments.

Obtrusive sounds

Noise can be a type of pollution which can actually cause harm as very loud noises can damage the eardrum. The class could discuss what noises they find pleasant and unpleasant and produce a questionnaire to find out whether other people hold the same opinions. This questionnaire could ask parents and other children about their likes and dislikes in the home as well as in the street; what noises prevent sleep or work; or how they would feel if there was no noise at all outside.

Ways of controlling noise could be considered. The children could place a clock or a battery-run radio in a box and try different ways of muffling the sound with materials like screwed up newspaper, wooden blocks, hay, foam pieces and fabric and then try to say which is most effective and why. As air does not carry sound as well as solid objects, springy things that are full of air holes will make better sound insulators than rigid objects. This may help children to appreciate why carpets and foam in cavity walls reduce noise. From their previous activities they may also be able to explain why wearing ear muffs when using loud machines reduces the sound. An experiment to find out their loss of hearing when using ear muffs, coat hoods and Walkman headphones might help the children to realize that muffling sound can be dangerous in some situations such as crossing the road or when riding bicycles.

The children could try to analyse the noises in the classroom with a view to reducing the noise levels. Initially they need to identify the noises and classify them into those that are disturbing or irritating and whether they are persistent or intermittent. Once the noises have been identified the children can make suggestions for action. These may include sticking small pieces of material or draught excluder to the inside of desk lids or cupboards, placing metal containers on carpet squares or newspaper, finding a piece of carpet for part of the classroom or producing a poster to encourage quieter behaviour.

FURTHER READING

Catherall, E. (1989) *Exploring Sound*. Hove: Wayland.

Department of Education and Science and the Welsh Office (1989) *Science in the National Curriculum*. London: HMSO.

Department of Energy *Energy in Primary Science: Unit 1. Mechanical Energy*, and *Unit 2. Sound*. London: Department of Energy.

Diamond, D. and Tiffin, R. (1976) *Teaching Primary Science: Musical Instruments*. London: Macdonald Educational.

Hutchinson, K. (1983) *Exploration Science: Air and Sound*. London: Evans.

Jennings, T. (1984) *The Young Scientist Investigates: Sounds*. Oxford: Oxford University Press.

Mares, C., Blanchard, H., Stephenson, R. and Redhead, M. (1988) *Our Environment: Teacher's Guide*. Walton-on-Thames: Thomas Nelson.

CHAPTER 8

Rocks and Soil

KEY STAGE 2
This chapter considers how children can investigate rocks, soils, and the processes of weathering and decomposition.

Investigating rocks and soils

In the primary school the main aim should be to help the children classify rocks and soils according to their features and properties. There is no requirement for the children, or the teacher, to be able to name a wide range of examples. By comparing different rocks the children should be able to develop some appreciation of how their properties are related to their formation and the way they can be used. It is sufficient for the children to be introduced to the three main types of rock formation, i.e. igneous, sedimentary and metamorphic, and a few of the most common examples of these, e.g. granite, basalt, clay, limestone, sandstone, marble and slate.

FINDING ROCKS IN THE ENVIRONMENT

If the children have not already studied the properties of building materials in detail they need some activities that will help them to distinguish between natural and man-made stone. Studies of their own school building should help to clarify the differences. This could be achieved by detailed annotated sketches of the exterior, identifying the appearance and type of the materials used. Most materials will be artificial, such as brick, concrete and mortar, but there may also be stone work, slates and pebbles in pebbledash concrete. Once the children can identify artificial materials easily they can explore the environment for examples of natural rock.

Table 8.1

Description of rock or stone	Place seen	Polished or rough	Signs of wear
Black, shiny, speckled	On steps of Post Office	Rough	Dip in step where feet have rubbed
Pale yellow and grainy	Walls of Council House	Rough	Corners broken, parts gone black
Pink, white and streaky	Pillars of office	Smooth Shiny	None
Yellow, sandy bits of stone and tiny shells	Garden wall	Rough	Cracked, with grass in the cracks

Many children who live in a large town or city may not have many opportunities to see outcrops of rocks or have the chance to visit quarries. However, a walk around a town or a visit to a graveyard are ideal places to see a variety of rocks. The children do not need to know what the rocks are at this stage. It is actually an advantage if they do not, as then they can research, test and classify the different rocks in a scientific way with open minds. Their observations and some detail about the rocks could be recorded as shown in Table 8.1.

If the children have the opportunity to look at gravestones the date of the stone can be added so that at a later date the children can investigate whether some rocks wear more than others. It may also be possible to arrange a visit to a stone mason who can demonstrate how the stones are used. It is important to bear in mind that builders use the term marble for any stone that can be polished. This is an interesting example of geologists and builders needing and using different classifications although using the same term.

If the children are involved in the collection of rock samples, subsequent investigations will have more meaning. They may be able to find pieces of rocks or pebbles in their garden, at the seaside or by the roadside. Where the school has easy access to the country the class could go out to collect samples from different locations. Each specimen can be washed and labelled with the location found and date of collection. This initial collection can be supplemented by ones already owned by the school or borrowed from a local secondary school or museum.

OBSERVING AND TESTING ROCKS

Initially the children can observe and describe the rocks as fully as possible. They might consider colour, texture, shape, feel and smell. The specimens may look different when wet. Magnifying lenses and microscopes should be available. If the children work in pairs and try to find out as many similarities and differences between only two rocks the observations are likely to be more detailed than if they attempt to look at many samples. The children are likely to come up with more ideas for comparison if the two rocks are significantly different. If the children are given different types of pencil, pastel colours and water colour paints they may also be able to produce a record of the pattern and colours of the rock by using a microscope.

Once the children have studied a few rocks in detail they should be able to suggest how they might classify them, such as in terms of colour, pattern, hardness and texture. They will probably be able to suggest some ways to test the rocks themselves. The teacher can use these ideas as a basis and suggest other things they might test. The class could design a table, similar to Table 8.2, to record their findings.

When the children consider the colours of the rock they might break off small pieces using a hammer, as long as it is not a precious museum specimen, to see the colours that have been unaffected by air, as the weathering process can change the colour. While using the hammer the rock should be covered with a cloth to stop pieces flying about and safety goggles worn to protect the eyes. The children will also be able to comment on how easily the rock breaks and whether it split easily along a natural cleavage. Slates, for example, split easily.

When the children look at the structure of the rock they may notice that some rocks are made of only one type of material whereas others are made of two or more constituents. If they look

Table 8.2

Characteristics	Rock 1	Rock 2
What colours can you see? 1. on the outside of the rock 2. on the inside after being broken		
Do bits break off easily?		
Does it split easily?		
Is it made of sand or tiny stones or angular interlocking bits?		
How many different sorts of bits are there? 1. seen with the naked eye 2. seen with a lens 3. seen with a microscope		
Does it contain fossils?		
Drop water on to the rock. Does the water soak in?		
Swish the rock about in water. Do any bits come off?		
What can it be scratched with?		
How heavy is it?		
Does it contain magnetic material?		
Does vinegar make it fizz?		

carefully they should see that some are angular or crystalline and others are more granular. Granite is an example of a rock with angular interlocking pieces. These rocks were originally molten and as they cooled crystals were formed. Sedimentary rocks, such as sandstone, are often made from granular fragments of broken rocks and sand cemented together. In these sedimentary rocks the bits of sand or tiny stones are still visible. Sedimentary rocks are also usually softer and more easily broken.

The children could try to develop their own test to assess the hardness of different rocks. They may suggest that they count the number of hits with a hammer needed to break the rock. If the hammer is not hit with the same effort on every occasion or if the stone breaks along a natural line of cleavage the test will not be fair, so the children will have to take this into account when designing their test. Hardness in rock usually refers to how easy it is to drill into. The children could, therefore, invent a scratch test. In this case they could collect different items that vary in their effectiveness for scratching. They might choose a plastic knitting needle, nail, coin and pencil. They first need to decide how to rank the scratchers. They might compare the depth of scratch produced on a piece of balsa wood. Once they have decided on a satisfactory set of scratchers they are then able to test the rocks. It is important to remember that the scratcher must cut into the surface, not just mark it.

If the children have already done some work on displacement and density (Chapter 10), they can calculate how heavy 1 cm^3 of each rock is. If the children are not told how to carry out the task at first the teacher will have the opportunity to assess whether the children can apply their previous knowledge and experiences to a new situation. The children first need to find the volume of a rock by lowering it into water and recording the displacement. If they then weigh the rock, they can work out what 1 cm^3 will be.

During work using compasses the class may have discussed the problem of distortion of the reading caused by rocks which contain iron. This is an opportunity to recap on that work by finding out whether any of the rocks are magnetic.

Rocks that are easily broken, or that can be dissolved by water or acid, are quickly weathered. The children can identify these rocks by watching whether bits often float away when the rock is swished about in water or whether the water becomes cloudy with suspended particles. The effect of acid can be ascertained by dropping vinegar on to the rock and watching to see if the surface bubbles and fizzes. Rocks containing calcium carbonate, such as chalk, marble and limestone, give off a gas when put with an acid. When rain contains a high level of acid, buildings made of these materials are easily weathered.

Once the children have tested their rocks they could discuss ways of classifying them into groups, trying to take into account several characteristics. At this point the teacher may wish to introduce the three main classifications used by geologists, i.e. metamorphic, igneous and sedimentary. Secondary sources will be needed to explain the differences.

TYPES OF ROCK

Igneous rocks, e.g. granite and basalt, are formed when molten material from inside the earth's crust reaches the surface, perhaps during volcanic activity, and cools. As the material cools the different minerals crystallize. Rocks that cool slowly have large crystals. The children can study the process of crystallization by making their own crystals. They could start by mixing salt into very warm water until the liquid is saturated, i.e. no more salt will dissolve. The solution is left to cool and evaporate leaving the crystals of salt. If the children try different substances, such as sugar, Epsom salts and lemonade powder, they should see different shapes of crystals under a microscope. In the same way different minerals in rocks form different types of crystals.

Sedimentary rocks are formed from existing rocks which have been worn away by the action of wind and water and from the bodies of small animals which have died. These pieces settle in layers at the bottom of seas and lakes and are compacted and cemented by other minerals. Sandstones are formed from sand; limestones from the remains of tiny shells and animals; shales from muds; and conglomerates are made from stones and rocks mixed with limestone or sandstone.

A series of 'sedimentary rocks' can be made by the children in an old plastic margarine box (Figure 8.1). They should partly fill the box with water and then add different layers of materials to

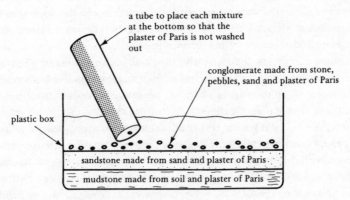

Figure 8.1 Making 'sedimentary' rocks

represent different types of sedimentary rock. Plaster of Paris is mixed in to all the different mixtures to act as a cementing mineral. For example, the mudstone is made of three parts soil and one part plaster of Paris. After setting, the layers can be removed from the box. Geologists use the fact that lower layers must have been laid down first in order to date rocks and fossils. This type of activity helps children to appreciate this idea.

Metamorphic rocks are rocks which have been changed due to great heat or pressure or both. Muddy shales are changed to slate and limestones to marble. When clay is fired in the school kiln the clays are changed in the same way.

FOSSILS

Fossils are traces of animals and plants that died millions of years ago, some of which are now extinct. Fossil remains are the only way scientists know some of these animals, e.g. dinosaurs, existed at all. Children at key stage 2 are expected to know that there are different ways of preservation. To understand this the children will need to look at samples of different types of fossil. It is unlikely that many children will have the opportunity to collect their own fossils. Not only are good examples fairly rare, but there is also an obligation not to damage the few good sites that exist. However, schools can buy facsimile fossils for the children to handle and they may also be able to borrow actual examples from museums or local secondary schools. As with the study of rocks the children should observe each specimen as carefully as possible and describe it and its possible life-style as fully as they can. Secondary sources will be required to extend their observations.

Some fossils are made by the original organism leaving a cast or mould of its shape or skeleton. Rocks made at the bottom of the sea often have fossils of this type in them. When an animal or plant dies it falls to the sea bottom and is covered with other material. The soft part of the animal decays and disappears leaving its shape, or impression, in the rock. This impression is sometimes filled with either mud or sand or by minerals. This new filling, or fossil, looks like the original shell, leaf or skeleton. The children can make their own 'fossil' in a similar way. A shell, twig or other item is pressed into clay to leave an impression. The space is filled with plaster of Paris. When it has set the 'fossil' can be removed.

Other plants and animals are preserved by a process of mineralization. The cells of the organisms are replaced by minerals. Sometimes pieces of wood are petrified in this way and if they are cut open the cell structure is still visible. Another method of fossilization occurred when amber was formed. Occasionally when a tree was damaged it secreted a resin. This sweet-smelling resin attracted insects which became trapped and preserved. Later the tree rotted and the hard resin remained. Some modern jewellery is made using a similar idea. A flower or other item is encased and preserved in plastic.

This introductory work on fossils could extend into studies on fossil fuels such as coal and oil; and on more recently extinct animals and those that are in danger of extinction.

Weathering

Rocks seem very permanent features in the world so children find it difficult to appreciate that they are slowly but constantly changing. The children need to see examples of the process in action and to understand how it occurs. During their study of rocks they may have noticed various clues indicating weathering has occurred. On a walk around a town they may have seen examples of materials that have changed since they were originally built, such as worn steps, cracks in walls and pavements, worn statues and carvings, and rusting metals. On a visit to a graveyard the clarity of carving and lettering can be compared on stones made of similar materials at different dates.

Using these examples the children can try to suggest ways that weathering could occur. Rocks can be broken up by being knocked together. The children may be able to suggest that this will occur in moving rivers, seas and high winds. Chemicals also change rocks as the children will have seen when they tested rocks with an acid like vinegar. Rocks are also split apart by the action of ice and by the action of plants (Chapter 13).

Investigating soils

As rocks are broken down they form soils; therefore different soils come from different types of rock. Soils consist not only of rock particles, but also of humus (broken-down plant or animal material), air and water. In sandy or gravel soil the rock particles are relatively large in size. Consequently it will be well drained, light and easy to work, but as the water drains through easily many chemical nutrients are washed away. Clay soils contain much smaller rock particles, so they drain badly and are difficult to dig but are often nutrient rich. Loams contain roughly equal amounts of sand and clay so are cultivated easily and contain a reasonable amount of nutrients. The children should investigate the properties of these three main types.

During key stage 2 the children are expected to have carried out an investigation of either rocks or soil. Investigations on soils may be included as part of studies on rocks and weathering or during an investigation of different localities and the ways in which plants and animals are suited to their location.

INVESTIGATING DIFFERENT TYPES OF SOIL

If at all possible the children should see where several layers of soil are exposed. A recently excavated hole on a building site or worn-away bank are possibilities. The children can then see that soil characteristics vary with depth. A soil profile can be made by gluing samples of the different layers on to a strip of wood to match with the original.

Different soils can be collected from the school grounds, supplemented by samples from the gardens of children and teachers. Different plant areas tend to produce different soil types, e.g. deciduous woods, coniferous woods, and open farmland. Ideally samples of clay, loams and sandy soils are required. The first activity needs to be very open-ended with the children trying to find out as much as possible for themselves by handling and observing the soils. They might comment on the differences in colour or smell; whether it feels wet, grainy, slippery, sticky or cold; if it contains stones of different sizes; if it is the home to many different creatures or has bits of plant material in it. Water and a variety of measuring equipment, lenses and microscopes could be available for some children to make up their own comparative tests. The children should decide how to record and report on their findings for themselves.

This initial exploration should enable the children to decide what are the major components of soil and to discuss with the teacher how they might test them further. Simple tests on proportion of different sized particles, amount of organic material, and differences in drainage and acidity are possible.

The comparative amounts of inorganic material (things that have never lived) and organic material can be seen by shaking samples of soil up in water and letting them settle. A glass or plastic jar, with a lid, should be half filled with one of the soil samples. The same volume of soil will be needed for each soil type so that the results are directly comparable. The jar is then filled with water until it is about three-quarters full. The jar is vigorously shaken and then left to settle overnight. The material will settle with the largest grains at the bottom. Any humus or organic matter, being lighter, will float on the top (Figure 8.2).

The depth of each layer can be measured and different soils compared. The pieces that float on the top can be removed and studied with a lens or microscope to see that they are mainly dead plant material. Another way to discover the proportions of particle sizes in different soils is to use a set of different meshed sieves. The children can discuss how to make the test fair. One way is to use samples of the same weight which have been allowed to dry out. The sieve with the largest mesh is used first. The soil is added, stirred and shaken, and the stones trapped in the sieve are weighed. Increasingly finer meshed sieves are used on what

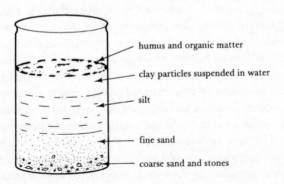

Figure 8.2 Observing comparative amounts of inorganic material and organic material

remains. Sandy soils will lose many of their particles during the first sieving but clay soils will have many very small particles.

A good soil for cultivation holds some water but still allows some drainage. The children may be able to think of a fair experiment to test which soils hold water best. One method is to dry out the soils first and then place samples of the same weight into similar dishes. The dishes and soil samples are weighed and then water is poured over the soils to fill the dishes. After letting the dishes stand for about three minutes the excess water is poured off, making sure no soil is lost in the process. The dishes are weighed again to discover how much water the soil has held. The children could also describe how the appearance of the soil has altered. If the samples are left for two or three days and re-examined, the children should see that clay soils easily become waterlogged, are very sticky when wet, and produce cracks as they dry out.

Different soils hold different amounts of air, depending on the size of the soil particles. The children initially can test the difference between large stones, gravel, small stones and sand. Four jars of the same size and volume are required. The jars are filled to the same level with the different samples. Water is then poured into the jars to fill them. The water is poured off into a measuring container and the amount recorded. More water will be needed if there were a lot of air spaces. Once the children understand the method they can test different soil samples in the same way. They must make sure that they do not press down or shake the soil samples as this will affect the air spaces.

Drainage can also be measured by timing the rate that water moves through a soil. The equipment is set up as shown in Figure 8.3.

The pot is filled with the soil sample. A measured amount of water is poured into the top of the soil. A stop-watch is used and started as soon as the first drop of water drains through. It is stopped when no water has dripped through for a minute. The children should be able to identify those soils that drain easily and quickly.

Some children may know that farmers and gardeners test their soils to find out whether their land is acidic or alkaline, as plants have different chemical requirements. One group of children, with careful supervision, could use a gardener's kit to test the soils.

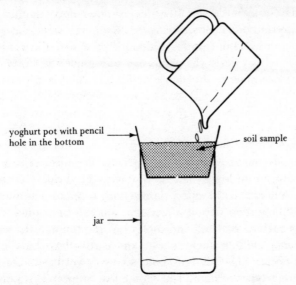

yoghurt pot with pencil
hole in the bottom

soil sample

jar

Figure 8.3 Investigating soil drainage

Different groups of children could carry out different tests and prepare reports for the rest of the class. They should always try to predict what will happen beforehand; to suggest improvements to their procedure; and to explain or make a hypothesis following the tests. The children could also consider how the different properties they notice might affect the growth of plants and animals. For example, when a soil is waterlogged animals and plant roots will not get air. Therefore they might make and test a hypothesis that soils that do not drain well will have fewer animals living in them than those that drain well.

From their discussions the children could predict and test which soil they think will be best to grow plants in. One way is to prepare pots of different soils with the same number of seeds and treat them in the same way. The success rate of germination, size and apparent health of the plants can then be compared. The children might try the experiment with different seeds, such as cress, lettuce and radish. The children may also test how effectively plants grow when the water condition of the same soil varies. In this case they need pots of the same soil and five seeds in each but each pot is watered in a different way. One pot might be given 10 ml every third day, another given 10 ml every other day, another 10 ml every day and one kept waterlogged. Again the success of growth can be recorded. Line graphs could be kept of the growth of shoots. After about two weeks the plants can be removed and roots, stem and leaf size measured in more detail.

CHANGING SOILS

Soils are changed naturally through the action of animals and artificially, to improve their productivity, by farmers. They can also be damaged by inappropriate action. Animals that live in the soil and how their action affects the soil can be studied. Large animals such as badgers and moles burrow through the soil but the smaller animals such as ants and earthworms have greater overall effect. The children could set up a wormery with layers of different types of damp soil. Some leaf litter and two or three worms should be placed on the surface. After a week or so the children should see that the layers are being mixed up by the action of the worms.

The children will have discovered that clay and sandy soils have disadvantages for growth. A farmer tries to reduce these disadvantages by digging and ploughing and adding fertilizer. Some children may have personal experiences about farming in Britain or other countries to add to the discussion.

The effect of digging can be demonstrated by comparing one soil that has been forked with one that has been left alone. The equipment can be set up as shown in Figure 8.4. One pot is dug with a fork each day. The children should find that less water is drawn up into this pot because air fills the spaces between the particles leaving less room for the water. Clay soils particularly benefit from regular digging.

Sandy soils on the other hand very quickly lose natural fertilizer. The children can test the effect of adding a fertilizer to seeds grown in sand compared to others without fertilizer. The way the fertilizer is used can also be assessed. Some pots could have the fertilizer mixed in with the sand and others have it sprinkled on the top. The effect of adding chemical fertilizer or weed-killer to the soil on animals that live there and the risk that some of the

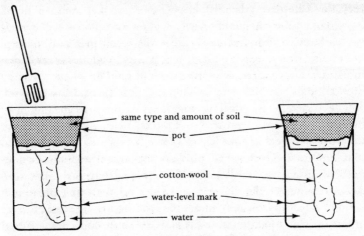

Figure 8.4 Investigating the effect of digging on soils

chemicals might be absorbed into the food produced could be discussed.

Just as soils can be improved they can also be damaged. The children should appreciate from their studies on weathering that soils take a very long time to be produced. Soils can be quickly damaged by contamination. The children could try the effect on seeds and growing plants when pollutants, such as oil, mild disinfectant or salt water, are added. If soil is left bare for long periods much of the top soil can wash or blow away. If dried soil is left outside on a windy day for a couple of hours the children will find that a lot blows away. They can find out how much by weighing it before and after taking it outside. This is a very serious problem in countries which have torrential rainfall or have very dry seasons.

Decomposing natural materials

A very fertile soil contains a lot of humus, which is the rotted remains of dead animals and plants. The children need to consider this process of decay and the factors that influence it, during key stage 2.

If the children have already considered the range of waste products produced by human activities and how they can be recycled (Chapter 3) they will know that some materials will break down over time but others such as glass and plastic will not. If the children review this work they will recall that only natural materials, from dead animals and plants, will decay and disintegrate. The teacher could ask the children if they have seen any dead animals and plants and what happens to them. Most children will have seen dead hedgehogs and foxes by the roadside and dead flowers and plants in gardens and parks. With a little prompting they will also realize that leaves that fall every autumn are dead plant material. The teacher could ask why this dead material does not continue to accumulate indefinitely and help the children to suggest examples they have seen of the decomposing process in action. The children may know that the bodies of dead animals are eaten by other animals. They will also have seen rotten vegetables or fruit with fungus. Decomposers include animals that eat dead plant material, animals that eat dead animals, fungi and bacteria.

The children could collect samples of leaf litter to study, ideally during the summer or autumn before the first frosts. They should collect not only the unaltered leaves on the surface but also the soil containing the decaying leaves. They could sort through the material carefully to collect, observe, draw and if possible identify the animals that they find. By observing the features and using books they may be able to identify which animals feed on plant material and which are carnivores. Secondary sources can be used to find out more about the food cycles. For example, worms, snails, millipedes, slugs and woodlice feed on dead leaves. These animals are the food for other animals such as birds and foxes. When the animals die their bodies are food for some types of beetles and maggots, which are food for other animals, and so on. The children can try to identify some food chains. It is important that the children realize that this constant recycling of natural material allows maximum use of the environment's resources. In the same way recycling man-made products can use the planet's limited resources economically.

Some of the decomposers, such as worms, woodlice and snails, can be kept in the classroom for a short time for detailed study. The eating preferences of an earthworm can be studied by placing different leaves on the top of the soil in a wormery and observing which are eaten. In the same way different leaves could be put in a box with a snail to find which are eaten and by how much. It is important that all animals are replaced in their original habitat. If possible a trip to a wooded or country area to try to find evidence not only of decomposers in the leaf litter but also of animal activity in fallen branches and fungus growth is helpful.

Fungi, including moulds and yeast, and bacteria are also decomposers. On the one hand it is important that children realize that bacteria are often useful, as in cheese and yoghurt making. On the other hand, however, great care must be taken with activities involving fungi and bacteria as some are dangerous. The children may be able to suggest the conditions they think would make things rot quickly and those that might slow the process. Their ideas could be used as the basis for comparing different conditions. Identical trays of different vegetable material, such as pieces of potato, cheese, orange, cabbage, apple, fallen leaves and bread, can be prepared but left in these different conditions. For example, one tray might be left dry and open to the air, another dry but covered with plastic film, another left damp and covered in film, another left damp and open to the air, another kept damp, uncovered and warm, and so on. The children can make observations of the daily changes of the different foods which have been left to rot in the trays. The children should not touch the items once the experiment has been set up. They should discover decay is more rapid in warm damp conditions which are open to the air so that spores can reach the food easily. Acidity, moisture content and available nutrients will determine which forms will appear. Because of the require-ments of safety, secondary sources will be required to study the factors of decay and decomposers of meat, such as the development of maggots, in more detail.

FURTHER READING

Collis, M. (1974) *Using the Environment 2: Investigations Part 2*. London: Macdonald Educational.

Collis, M. and Kincaid, D. (1982) *Learning through Science: Out of Doors*. London: Macdonald.

Department of Education and Science and the Welsh Office (1989) *Science in the National Curriculum*. London : HMSO.

Children and Primary Science

Jennings, T. (1982) *The Young Scientist Investigates: Rocks and Soil*. Oxford: Oxford University Press.

Mares, C., *et al.* (1988) *Our Environment: Teachers Guide*. Walton-on-Thames: Thomas Nelson.

Mares, C., *et al.* (1988) *Our Environment: Workcards*. Walton-on-Thames: Thomas Nelson.

Millyard, J. and Smithers, C. (1981) *Science Horizons. Level 1: Soil, Seeds and Trees*. London: Macmillan.

Radford, D. (1973) *Change: Stages 1 and 2 and Background*. London: Macdonald Educational.

Richards, R. and Kincaid, D. (1983) *Learning through Science: Earth*. Hemel Hempstead: Macdonald.

Richards, R. and Kincaid, D. (1985) *Exploring: Cycles: Soil Cycles*. Cambridge: Cambridge University Press.

CHAPTER 9

Earth and Atmosphere

KEY STAGE 2
This chapter considers how children can investigate variations in weather. Some practical activities intended to help children to understand day and night, phases of the moon and the place of the planet Earth in the context of the solar system are also examined.

The weather and its effects

In the early years the children should have become aware of the changing seasons and the variations of weather throughout the year. During key stage 2 they can build on their experiences to study the weather in greater depth by designing and using devices to make comparative and quantitative observations. These measurements may include changes of temperature, precipitation, and wind direction and strength.

Studies of weather variations enable children to collect data and to collate it in different ways to look for patterns and relationships. When the children try to explain these patterns they are enabled to make simple hypotheses and predictions which are then testable. The design of devices to measure precipitation and wind strength and directions involves children in studying the variations of the wind's action and rainfall in open-ended, problem-solving situations. When children have the experience of making measuring instruments they become more aware of the need to select instruments for specific tasks.

TEMPERATURE

The teacher might ask the children to find the warmest and coolest place in the school grounds at different times of the day. The whole

143

class may discuss the problem to share ideas, and then small groups could plan where and when they intend to collect the data. The children might consider different heights above the ground, different times of day, locations over different ground surfaces, areas in sunshine and shadow, places near the school compared to open spaces and walls facing in different directions. Once the data have been collected the children can be involved in deciding how to record and compare the information. This might be in the form of charts, graphs and/or by using maps.

As soon as the warmest and coldest places have been identified the children can be asked to try and explain the differences. They are likely to suggest several hypotheses, such as the coldest spots are in windy places; and the warmest places are near the school walls because heat from the school warms the adjoining air. Predictions based on each hypothesis can be made and different groups can collect further data to support or disprove them.

Temperatures could be recorded over a few weeks at regular times of the day and compared with information collected on wind direction and rainfall. The children can again attempt to interpret the data to suggest connections between the sets of data. It is important that the teacher is aware that data collection is only part of a process that either aims to raise questions for further study or is intended to answer a problem or to test a hypothesis. Data collection as an end in itself is insufficient.

The children may have noticed that temperatures vary on different ground surfaces and at different heights above the ground surface. The teacher may wish to follow this up in more detail. If the children fill two similar containers with water and soil respectively, place them in the sun and then record the temperature changes at hourly intervals they should discover water is very slow to heat and then later to cool. Children may recall that on visits to the seaside the sea feels cold but the sand feels hot. This is an important experience as later children will learn that the difference in temperatures of large water areas, such as the sea and lakes, have important influences on air movements.

These activities may help children to realize why national weather data need to be collected in the same way all over the country. Data have to be collected in a special box which has slatted sides to keep the instruments in the shade but still allow air movement. The box has to be fixed at the same height above the ground surface. (Further activities investigating thermometers and their use can be found in Chapter 13.)

PRECIPITATION

An open-ended problem to design and make a device to collect and measure rainfall will involve the children in scientific and technological skills. The first part of the problem is to find a suitable container to collect rain. The children could put out many different containers, e.g. buckets, tins, yoghurt pots, plant pots, bottles, boxes and trays, in the rain to judge which are inappropriate and why. They could be tested in different conditions such as in showers, wind and in stormy weather. If necessary, different weather conditions may have to be simulated by using watering cans. Some containers will not catch or hold water effectively, others overflow easily, some fall over, and it will not be possible to see the level of the water in order to measure it in others. The merits and disadvantages of each container can be considered in order to decide on the ideal size and shape.

In order to prompt the children to consider improving the device the teacher may need to raise different problems. For example the children can be asked to consider how to reduce water loss by evaporation or how to stop water splashing into the device and making the results inaccurate. If the children have not studied evaporation the teacher will have to introduce it at this stage. The children first need to check whether evaporation will influence their results. If they measure out equal amounts of water into similar containers they can measure the loss of water when it is left in very warm places, in a sheltered sunny spot, compared to a windy exposed place, and a sheltered cool place. As the rate of evaporation will vary in these places the children should appreciate that they need to reduce the evaporation in their rain gauge. They need some type of cover which still enables the rain to be collected effectively, e.g. a funnel.

The children might notice that when the rain hits the ground it splashes upwards. This splash may cause extra water to fall into the rain gauge. The children need to reduce this by devising either some splash guard or raising the opening of the device above the

145

usual splash level. A watering can is very useful for creating 'rainfall' for testing purposes. The children also need to think of a way to ensure that the device is stable and will not be blown over.

After the shape has been improved the children could consider how to read how much rain has fallen. Will they need to remove the water to measure it or can they calibrate and mark the outside of the device? One possible solution is shown in Figure 9.1.

The children finally should decide where to place the rain gauge. They can use their gauges and locate them in different places around the school to record the differences in water collected. Those with a lot of rain or very little rain are likely to be false results, because they have either been sheltered or been in a location where extra water drips in. After going through this process of design and make the children will be a better position to appraise manufactured rain gauges.

Rain is not the only form of precipitation. If the occasion arises work can be done on snow. Discussion can take place about what snow is like; what the sky is like when it is about to snow; why snow is deeper in some places rather than others; how snow is cleared

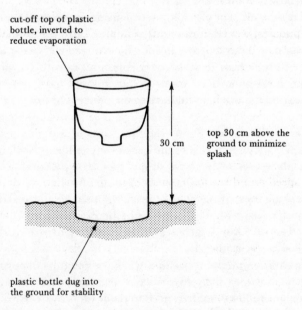

Figure 9.1   A rain gauge made from a plastic bottle

from the roads; and why the sea rarely freezes. Individual snow flakes can be observed with a lens or microscope and the children can compare fresh snow with old and trodden snow. (See Chapter 13 for further experiments on ice and evaporation.)

SUNSHINE AND CLOUD COVER

A simple cloud reflector can be made to help the children to identify different types of clouds and to estimate cloud cover. An old picture frame with glass in it is required. If the picture is replaced by black paper the frame can be placed on the ground and the clouds will be reflected in it. It enables the children to watch and draw the shape and movements of the clouds without constantly having to strain to look upwards. The children can try to estimate the cloud cover and draw common cloud forms and try to work out what sort of weather is usually associated with them. They may try a simple classification and then compare their classification with that produced in books or by the Meteorological Office.

Studies on clouds can develop into how moisture gets into the air or how it comes out, or is precipitated. The children can be asked to think of their own examples of moisture going into air, e.g. from puddles, wet clothes, ponds, a boiling kettle and breath seen on a cold day. They may suggest condensation of water on windows or on a plate held in steam as examples of moisture coming out of the air. Very able children will be able to build up an understanding of the water cycle from these types of activities.

WIND DIRECTION AND SPEED

One of the most effective ways of interesting children in measuring wind speed and direction is to set them the problem of designing and making their own devices. Groups of children could research, plan, make and evaluate either a device to measure wind direction or wind speed. Children find thinking of ideas for measuring wind direction easier as they have usually noticed flags and wind socks at airports, or weather vanes. They will have to solve many design problems such as choosing suitable light material fixed on a triangular support arrangement for a wind sock; making a flag and pole stable by perhaps fixing it into a bottle weighted with sand;

or finding a shape for a weather vane so that it turns appropriately into the wind.

The children may have difficulties thinking up ideas for a device (anemometer) to measure wind speed. Use of reference material can sometimes avoid giving children valuable first-hand experiences but it can, as in this case, be used to prompt ideas, support and extend work. Three possible designs are suggested in Figure 9.2.

The children might compare their models with manufactured anemometers. The children could also look at the Beaufort scale. The Beaufort scale is a 13-point scale for judging wind speed including '0 Calm', which is defined as when smoke rises vertically; '7 Moderate gale', where whole trees are in motion and the wind is difficult to walk against; to a final point of '12 Hurricane' force winds. In some city areas the children are unlikely to see smoke and may not have many trees nearby so they could be asked to make their own modernized version suitable for their particular area.

Using manufactured anemometers the children could find out how the wind speed and direction vary around the school because of the shape of the building. The aim of the survey could be to find the best place to have a picnic, play cards, fly a kite, and dry washing. As wind is always gusting and changing direction the children need to work in twos. One child needs to take a measurement in open ground to find the prevailing wind direction while the other measures the wind in, different locations so that each pair of recordings can be compared.

During their own studies of weather conditions the children could compare their records with those produced by the media. They might collect different sources of weather information in newspapers, taped radio reports and videoed television forecasts. They could discuss both the style and effectiveness of presentation as well as their accuracy.

A number of the activities involved with measuring weather differences take some time. It is probably not feasible for every child to try all the activities. However, different groups could be given different investigations or tasks and be expected to share and report their findings to their peers.

paper cups fixed to wooden sticks

The wind catches the cups and turns the device. The number of complete turns per minute is recorded. If one cup is painted red, counting is easier.

beads to enable the cups to turn easily

stick

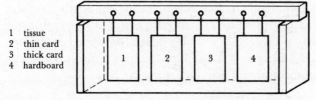

1 tissue
2 thin card
3 thick card
4 hardboard

A light wind will only move the tissue whereas a strong wind will move all the pieces of material.

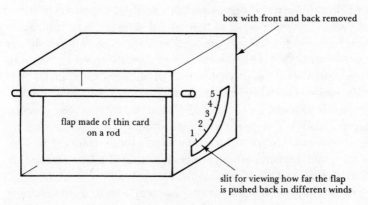

box with front and back removed

flap made of thin card on a rod

slit for viewing how far the flap is pushed back in different winds

Figure 9.2 Devices to measure wind speed

The Earth as a planet

Although most junior children will say that the Earth is round because of the information they have gained from the television and other media, some find it difficult to accept. In their experience the Earth is flat and the skyline horizontal. In these cases the children often hold two views simultaneously: the official and their alternative. They may attempt to reconcile the two by different strategies. When asked to explain why others say the Earth is round, suggestions include saying that it is round and flat surrounded by an ocean; or that as hills and mountains are rounded the Earth is described as round; or that there is a sphere between themselves on the ground and the sky above. Yet other children may think of the Earth as a huge ball with people living inside on a flat surface with the sky above as the upper hemisphere. If the teachers are aware of possible difficulties the children's views can be discussed and questioned sensitively. Much of a topic studying the Earth as a planet must inevitably depend on secondary sources, making re-adjustment of the children's views difficult. However, there are some practical activities that may help.

DAY AND NIGHT

A comparison of day and night can initiate curiosity about diurnal changes. This might be initiated by considering nocturnal animals and their life-style; different people's feelings expressed in terms of prose or poetry; types of lights used at night; and comparing how well different colours are seen at night. The children do not usually ask why it is dark at night, but once the question has been raised they are usually fascinated. The children could make their own suggestions which can be compared with past religious and academic explanations. Scientific ideas and hypotheses depend on available knowledge and technical equipment. Consequently science is not a static subject and is subject to constant review, testing and adjustment. It is important that children realize that they can be part of this development.

Most children of junior school age are aware, from watching television, that the Earth orbits around the sun, but they do not understand how this effects the change of day and night. This can be demonstrated by using a lamp, OHP or projector light. One child stands in the light and slowly turns around. As this happens the class will see that sometimes the child's face is in shadow and sometimes in the direct light. The children should be able to see that one complete turn is the equivalent to one day and night. A globe can then be placed in the light and turned round. The children can note when different parts of the world, such as Britain, Pakistan, West Indies, North America and Africa, are in 'daylight'. Children who are in contact with relatives in other countries should be able to confirm that they have different times. They might make pictures of what children around the world are doing at any one time.

PHASES OF THE MOON

It is important to start with the children's knowledge and experiences. Most children have some knowledge or views about the moon. The moon is particularly significant in some religions, e.g. Islam. Primary children appear to be able to hold conflicting beliefs simultaneously. For example, many children 'know' that the surface of the moon is covered with dust and craters from watching television; but also are convinced that they see a real 'man in the moon'. This represents the gradual change from a fictional or mythological explanation to a more accepted scientific idea, which is very slow when the concepts are abstract. The children need as many experiences as possible to enable this slow development to progress. They can read and discuss both fiction and non-fiction books about the moon. The children can be set the problem of making a model of the moon's surface as accurately as possible, referring to secondary sources. Lunar modules and rockets might be included.

To enable the children to understand why the moon appears to change its shape a lamp can be used in a similar way as before. On this occasion two children are needed. One represents the Earth. As the moon has no heat energy of its own we see light from it when it reflects the sun's light. To represent this idea the child representing the moon could hold a round mirror against her chest. Only one side of the moon faces the direction of the Earth. The moon-child should move slowly around the Earth-child, facing the Earth the whole time. The watching class should see that sometimes the

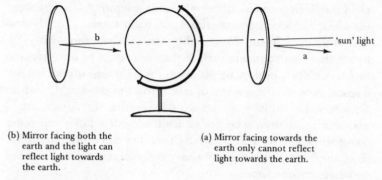

(b) Mirror facing both the earth and the light can reflect light towards the earth.

(a) Mirror facing towards the earth only cannot reflect light towards the earth.

Figure 9.3 Experiment to show why the moon 'changes shape'

mirror is in shadow and cannot reflect light from the lamp. As the child moves around the 'Earth', more light will be reflected by the mirror (Figure 9.3).

The children have difficulties appreciating the sizes and distances involved. They see that the moon appears bigger than the sun or stars; so they understandably think that it is. Perception of distance is another concept that takes years to develop. Several experiences can assist however. The children can be given a coin and a plate. The plate is placed at a distance and the children hold the coin close to their eyes. The coin looks bigger but they know from experience that the plate is bigger. On another occasion the children could have two identical torches. If they hold one close it will look far bigger than the one giving a pinprick of light from the far end of the corridor. The children can also discuss things that they can see at a distance through the window. Do the houses really get smaller as they get further away? Children who have flown in aeroplanes may remember how small houses looked from the air. The children could also place poles, of the same height, at different distances from the school to see how their height appears to change.

STARS AND THE SOLAR SYSTEM

An imaginary space trip could extend the work into considering the Earth's place in the solar system. The relative positions of the planets in the solar system can be discovered by the children using books. Then different children can take on the role of each planet and orbit one child in the centre as the sun. Additional children could be moons and circle the appropriate planets. This activity will help the children to realize that planets further out take longer to orbit the sun. Very able children could research the distances of the planets and position their friends or make a model showing the relative distances. Using people as a working model needs a lot of space. A very large playground or a trip to a nearby park may be necessary.

The nearest star is 24 million miles away and it takes four light years for its light to reach Earth. The children could find out the speed of different items, such as a runner, car, Concorde, rocket, and make a chart of comparative speeds so that they can have some idea of how fast light travels. They might find out how long it has taken different space probes to get to different planets in the solar system and prepare an imaginary journey to others.

Children find it very difficult to understand that stars do not only come out at night but are there all the time, but cannot be seen. This can be explained by asking the children to compare a torch in a bright light and one in a dark room. The torch is the same, it does not shine any more brightly but the contrast makes it appear brighter and is easier to see. The children can be asked to look for particular constellations when they go home at night. This could be followed up by discussions on how the position of the stars can be used for navigation.

Many children will not understand all the concepts of distance and relationships of planets and stars in their primary school years but if the activities have been practical with a view to starting them to think about their perception of distances and speeds they will have a good foundation for further work in the secondary school. The very exotic nature of the subject excites and stimulates many children who explore the ideas further for themselves. When a topic catches the interest of the children they will persist in trying to understand difficult ideas and in fact will revel in them.

FURTHER READING

Catherall, E. (1981) *Wind Power*. Hove: Wayland.

Collis, M. (1974) *Using the Environment: 2. Investigations Part 2*. London: Macdonald Educational.

Collis, M. and Kincaid, D. (1982) *Learning through Science: Out of Doors*. London: Macdonald.

Department of Education and Science and the Welsh Office (1989) *Science in the National Curriculum*. London: HMSO.

Driver, R., Guesne, E. and Tiberghien, A. (eds) (1985) *Children's Ideas in Science*. Milton Keynes: Open University Press.

Green, C. and James, R. (1985) *Investigating Weather*. Leeds: E.J. Arnold.

Gordon-Smith, C. (1981) *Science Horizons. Level 1: From Rain to Tap. West Sussex Science 5–14 Scheme*. London: Macmillan Educational.

Jennings, T. (1982) *The Young Scientist Investigates: Water*. Oxford: Oxford University Press.

Jennings, T. (1988) *Into Science: Weather*. Oxford: Oxford University Press.

Mills, D. (ed) (1981) *Geographical Work in Primary and Middle Schools*. Sheffield: The Geographical Association.

Radford, D (1973) *Change: Stages 1 and 2 and background*. London: Macdonald Educational.

Richards, R. and Kincaid, D. (1983) *Learning through Science: Earth*. Hemel Hempstead: Macdonald.

CHAPTER 10
Exploring Forces

KEY STAGE 2
Ideally, young children will have played with toys and explored their movement. Hopefully they will have become familiar with the idea that objects need an energy source to move and understand that pushes and pulls can make things start moving, speed up, swerve or stop. Junior children can build on this foundation to understand and investigate specific forces. This chapter considers gravity, upthrust in liquids, air and water resistance, and friction in detail.

What are forces?

In physics and engineering a force is either a push or a pull. This push or pull has the effect of attracting or repelling things, speeding them up or slowing them down. Forces do not always act in a straight line. They can also make things change their direction of motion. For example, the rudder on a boat, by pushing against the water, moves the boat in a new direction.

Children often have difficulty differentiating between the concepts of force and energy, probably because both are abstract concepts and are assumed by the child to be related to moving things. A force is a push or pull, whereas energy is what makes things happen or change. Children usually imagine that forces belong to something that is actively moving. They see the bulldozer pushing earth away, another child pulling on a rope, or the ball bouncing off the wall. It is difficult for the children to appreciate abstract forces acting on objects that may not even cause movement. There is also an erroneous tendency to assume only one force is acting in any one situation. For example, a motionless book on a table is being affected by gravity pulling down on it while the table is exerting a force upwards. A car which is moving is affected by several forces, including gravity, friction and air resistance. By providing plenty of guided practical experiences the teacher can help the children to gradually replace any misconceptions and to clarify their understanding.

The common forces that the children can investigate are:

- *Weight*. The pull of gravity on an object.
- *Magnetic force*. Magnets pull or attract iron objects. They also push or repel each other (Chapter 6).
- *Electrostatic force*. A rubbed plastic comb attracts water from a tap, or picks up little pieces of paper with an electrostatic force.
- *Upthrust*. Air bubbles rise in water. The water pushes them up with an upward force. If a cork is held under water it is possible to feel the water pushing it upwards.

As well as forces that cause movement, there are forces that stop or reduce movement, such as air and water resistance and friction.

- *Air resistance* pushes against moving cars and aircraft and makes them travel more slowly. Parachutes use this drag force.
- *Water resistance* slows the movement of boats and ships.
- *Frictional forces* act when two surfaces rub against each other, making it more difficult for the surfaces to slide over each other.

Measuring forces

Forces are measured in newtons. A newton meter is a type of spring balance and can be used to measure forces of between about 0.1 N and 100 N. Some spring balances show both kilograms and newtons. The children can see that as they pull on the spring balance they need to pull harder or exert more force to show a high reading. Because gravity is the force of the Earth's pull, newtons and grams are related, i.e. the pull of 100 grams is the same as 1 newton.

Gravity and stability

GRAVITY

From the time babies drop their toys out of their prams, or try to stand, they become aware that the Earth pulls things. The children could be asked to think of examples that demonstrate the existence of gravity. They might suggest that when an object rolls off a table it falls downwards; or that water squeezed out of a bottle falls down; or that when a ball is thrown, eventually it falls downwards.

Every object exerts a force of attraction, but usually it is so small we do not notice. The greater the mass, the greater is its pull. This pull is usually only significant when huge masses, like planets, are involved. To help the children clarify where the force of gravity is acting from, the teacher could ask them to suggest what is happening in another part of the world. Do objects still fall downwards? Children who have visited other countries will be able to give their experiences. Model figures fixed on different locations on a globe might help the children to see that gravity pulls towards the centre of the Earth. The concept can be further explained by tying a ball on to a string and whirling it around. The Earth's pull acts a little like the string. Occasionally children ask why the moon is not pulled onto the Earth. Again this can be explained by using the ball on the string. As the children whirl the ball around they should feel it pull outwards. If they let go the ball would fly off. To keep the moon in its orbit there is a balance of forces. Gravity pulls the moon towards the Earth but a second force, the centrifugal force, is pulling it outwards.

Measuring weight is actually a measurement of the Earth's gravitational pull. This explains why a spring balance can measure both kilograms and newtons. Each object has a mass which is made up of an amount of material. This is not the same as volume, because the volume can be changed by squashing or compressing it, but mass cannot be changed. Each child's weight is the amount of gravitational force which is pulling on their mass.

The nearer the centre of the force, the stronger is its effect. The further into space you go, the weaker the gravitational force becomes. The children can be reminded that they have already met this idea when using magnets and static electricity. If a magnet is lowered on to a paper-clip the magnetic force between them gets steadily stronger. Eventually the paper-clip will jump to the magnet. This also occurs with electric fields where electrostatic forces are acting. If the children rub a balloon it can pick up pieces of paper even when the balloon is not touching the paper.

Although this idea is difficult for children to understand, now space capsules are common, they are aware that they have weight on Earth but are 'weightless' in space and they would have less weight on the moon. Gravity depends on the mass of each planet. A large planet, like the Earth, has a stronger gravity than a smaller body like the moon. On the moon our mass stays the same but our weight changes. The moon's gravitational pull is about one-sixth that of Earth because it is smaller. Therefore our weight will be one-sixth of our Earth weight.

DO ALL THINGS FALL AT THE SAME RATE?

If a heavy steel ball bearing and a glass marble of the same size are dropped together on to a metal tray it should be possible to hear that they hit the tray at the same time. Ideally the children should stand on a chair to increase the height of drop. The activity needs to be repeated several times to confirm the result. This experience is most convincing when the drop is quite considerable, such as from a high building or bridge. However, such opportunities are rarely available to primary schools.

It is important to be careful with the choice of objects. Air resistance will affect light objects. Once the children understand that all things fall at the same rate they might investigate the effect of air resistance. Its effect can be easily demonstrated by comparing the fall of a sheet of paper with a similar piece screwed up into a tight ball. This could lead to work on parachutes, gliders and how animals, e.g. birds and bats, have used this principle.

STABILITY

Unstable objects are easily pulled over by the pull of the earth's gravity. A few simple activities can be set up to help children find the factors that influence stability. The children could be asked to build a tall tower out of bricks or old boxes and then asked to explain what factors helped to make the tallest tower?

The children could also carry out a simple shake test to classify objects into stable and unstable. A variety of items can be balanced

Table 10.1

Object	Estimate (stable/unstable)	First test	Second test	Third test
cup		stable	unstable	stable
flat ruler		stable	stable	stable
standing toy giraffe		unstable	unstable	unstable

on a flat tray or board. The tray is then gently shaken. The items that fall down are marked as unstable and those that stayed upright are marked as stable. A test of this type will also enable the teacher to emphasize the importance of repeating the experiment. The children can record their predictions and findings in a table like the one shown in Table 10.1.

Once the children have sorted the objects they can try to decide what features are common to all the very stable items, or to all the unstable objects. They can then make a hypothesis to explain stability. They might say things are stable because they are heavy. They are then able to test their hypothesis by collecting a set of heavy things and a set of light things to test as before to see if their prediction was correct.

After such activities the children will probably identify that a large heavy base makes the object stable. They can further clarify or test these ideas by using small identically sized boxes, e.g. match boxes, for further investigation. Each group of children can be given three boxes. The same amount of plasticine should be put at the bottom of one box; in the middle of another; and at the top of the third. The first box is placed, standing up, on the board. The board is slowly lifted until the box falls off and the height of instability is recorded (Figure 10.1). The test needs to be repeated three or four times to ensure the results are consistent. The other two boxes are tested in the same way. The children should discover that the lower the weight the more stable the object.

A similar activity can test the importance of the size of base. On this occasion all three boxes are filled with plasticine to make them heavy. They are then glued on to the centre of different sized cards. One box could have no base; another a base 4 cm × 4 cm; and the third might have a base of 6 cm × 6 cm.

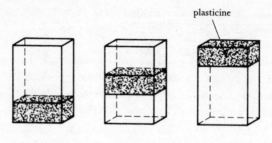

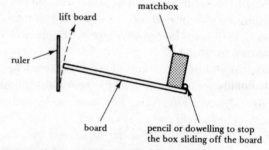

Figure 10.1 Investigating whether the position of weight in an object makes any difference to its stability

The board is used in the same way as before. Each box is tested and the point of instability is recorded. The children should find that as the base increases in size the box becomes more stable. Able children could try to find if there is a relationship between size of base and angle of instability. Instead of using a ruler a protractor is used. They would need to measure the angle for boxes with no base and bases of 4 cm, 9 cm, 16 cm, 25 cm, etc. This activity has the added advantage of enabling the children to see the mathematical relationship between the increasing angle and increasing height.

APPLYING THE IDEA OF STABILITY

The children need to see when stability is an important consideration. For example, people are allowed to stand downstairs on a bus but not upstairs where they would make the bus unstable. Babies'

160

high chairs must be stable so that they do not tip over when the baby leans out. When young children are present it is important to have stable furniture so that it is not knocked over. The children might collect pictures of furniture and set them into stable and unstable; or design a safe room for a crawling baby.

Some toys, e.g. a wobbly clown, are so stable that they return to their original position after being knocked over. The children could be asked to invent a way of making a wobbly doll. They might use half a ball filled with plasticine with the doll shape on top. A bottle with a rounded bottom and sand at the base or half a potato with a balsa-wood figure are other methods.

Manufactured goods can be compared for stability. The children might investigate which mugs or shampoo bottles are the most stable. The mugs or bottles could be tested full, half full and empty. This type of investigation can involve testing other properties such as capacity or whether the mugs can retain heat but still be safe to hold. Finally the children might design the ideal mug.

FINDING THE CENTRE OF GRAVITY

An object behaves as though all its weight is concentrated at one point. This is the centre of gravity. The position of this point determines whether or not the object will topple over. If the centre of gravity is vertically over the base of the object it will be stable. Once the centre of gravity is vertically outside the base the object will topple over. The children can discover this for themselves.

They first need to be able to find the centre of gravity of an object. Using 2D material simplifies the task considerably. A quick method is to balance a ruler or piece of card on a finger or pencil tip. The point of balance is the centre of gravity. A more accurate method is to use a plumb line. The children need to be provided with some fairly large regular and irregular shaped pieces of card. Three holes are made, anywhere near the edges of the shape. The children should put a nail through one hole. Hang a plumb line, of thin string and a washer, from the nail and draw the position of line of the string on the card (Figure 10.2a). This should be done for all three points. Where the lines meet is the point of balance (Figure 10.2b). The children can check that it is the balance point.

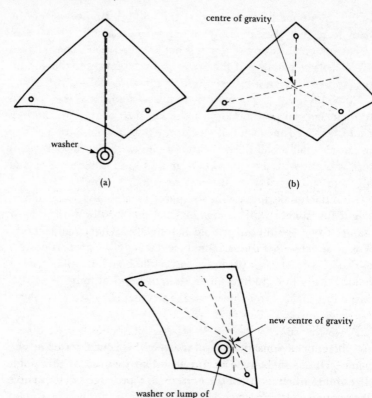

Figure 10.2 Finding the centre of gravity of an irregular shaped card

The effect of changing the mass of the card can be explored. Once the centre of gravity has been found, a piece of plasticine or washer can be sellotaped on to the card (Figure 10.2c). Can the children estimate where the new centre of gravity will be? They can then test their prediction.

This idea can be applied to a ship's cargoes or ballast. This time the shape of a ship is used and the centre of gravity found. Using the tilt boards the ship is tilted until it becomes unstable. The children should note where the centre of gravity is at the point of

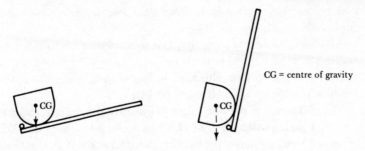

CG = centre of gravity

The pull downwards from the centre of gravity is above the board. Therefore the shape will stay on the board.

The pull downwards from the centre of gravity is beyond the end of the board. The shape will now fall off the board.

Figure 10.3 Investigating the relationship between the centre of gravity and the point of instability

instability and try to make up a rule that explains when an object becomes unstable (Figure 10.3).

A weight, either a washer or piece of plasticine, can be placed in different positions of the ship outline. The new centre of gravity can be found and then the outline tested for the point of instability. The children can use these observations to work out advice to give the captain of a ship when loading a boat.

Stability in the design of boats is very important. If they are badly designed they will capsize. The importance of the keel can be demonstrated by loading boats made out of plastic cups or margarine containers. An empty plastic cup will tend to float on its side. If the children add small weights to it they should discover that as the weights are added the cup becomes upright. This is the same effect as a keel on a boat. The children will also discover that loading the cup unevenly or overloading it will make it more likely to capsize.

A more open-ended exploration can be developed by giving the children rectangles of balsa wood to a scale that fits in with the size of a cocktail-stick mast, and asking them to find as many ways as possible to make their boat unstable. They might try loading the mast, making the boat narrower or shorter or changing the position of the mast. Once they have done this they can make a series of hypotheses, e.g. narrow boats are unstable because the base is small, which can then be tested.

Another problem-solving activity to stimulate discussions on stability is to give the children a prepared boat. The boat must be narrow enough so that although it floats upright it will capsize easily when blown along (Figure 10.4a).

The children can then be asked to improve the design. Pictures of actual yachts will help. The children could add a weighted keel (Figure 10.4b) or change the boat into a catamaran. In the first case they are lowering the centre of gravity and in the second increasing the size of the base to increase stability. During their activities they may also discover that if the mast is not fairly central the boat is likely to capsize. The weight of the mast causes the centre of gravity to be off-centre and as the boat sways on the water the centre of gravity is likely to moved beyond the base of the boat so it becomes unstable.

Forces in water

DISPLACEMENT IN WATER

When an object is put into a liquid the water level rises or is displaced. Aesop's story of the crow and the pitcher is one way to introduce the topic. The children might also discuss what happens to the water level when they get in and out of the bath.

The children need time to explore this for themselves. They could be given a container and various objects and asked to predict

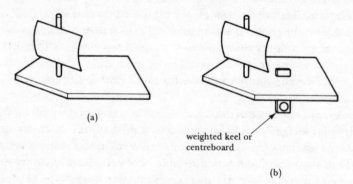

(a)

weighted keel or
centreboard

(b)

Figure 10.4 Stability in the design of boats

what will happen to the water when they drop something into the jar. They should drop things in and mark the level, then remove the objects and discuss what has happened. The teacher might ask the children to notice what happens if they put a big or small item in the water. Unit cubes that fix together enable the investigation to be extended. If different shapes made with the same number of cubes are put into water the children should find that the water rises by the same amount for each, showing that the shape of the objects that sink is not significant because their volumes and displacements are the same.

The children might then be given a variety of balls of different sizes and shapes and asked to find the volume of the balls by using displacement. They need to choose a suitable container to fit the size of the ball. Then they need to find a suitable method: collecting the overflow; seeing how much the water rises when adding a ball; or seeing how much it drops when the ball is removed. By setting a problem of this type the children will get experience of choosing appropriate equipment and measuring method. Obviously the method and container needed to measure a marble is different from that required for a football.

During the activities the children should also have noticed that they needed to push objects that floated below the surface. If an object floats it does not displace all its volume unless it is deliberately pushed below the surface.

UPTHRUST

Water pushes upwards on all objects. Children might have noticed that when they walk into the sea they feel as though they are lifted off the ground by the water. They might notice how difficult it is to hold a cork under the water.

The effect of upthrust can be measured by using a spring balance. When an object is weighed in air and then in water the reading on the spring balance will show a lower second reading (Figure 10.5). If the children record their findings in a table such as the one shown in Table 10.2 they should see a pattern emerge. They should find the spring balance always shows a lower reading when the object is in water as the upthrust acts against the force of gravity. The reading will be zero for objects that float because

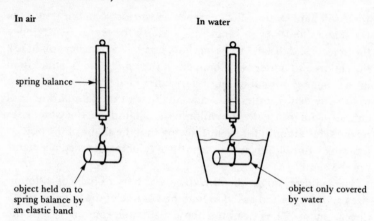

In air

In water

spring balance ⟶

object held on to
spring balance by
an elastic band

object only covered
by water

Figure 10.5   Investigating the effect of upthrust using a spring
balance

Table 10.2

Object	Reading in air	Reading in water	Float/sink
stone	530 gm	306 gm	sink
block of wood	345 gm	0 gm	float
bottle filled with sand	— gm	— gm	—

the water's upthrust is greater than the force of gravity.

More able children can try to find out the relationship between
the amount of upthrust and the displaced water. They should find
the reading in air, the reading in water, and the amount displaced
by an object that sinks. This activity needs very careful measurements. Again if the children record their results they should see a
pattern. When the object sinks, the difference shown on the spring
balance between the object in air and suspended in water should
be the same as the amount of displaced water. The support that the
object gets from the water is equal to the weight of the water that
the object pushes aside and upwards.

Another similar activity can be set up as shown in Figure 10.6

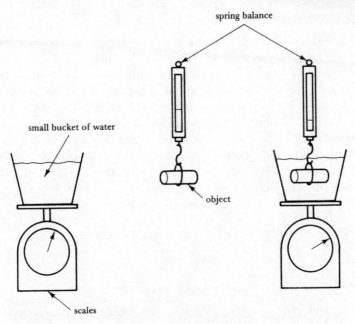

Figure 10.6 Investigating the effect of upthrust using a spring balance and scales

and data collected for a table, such as the one shown in Table 10.3, in order to look for a pattern in the results.

The difference of readings on the scales between the bucket of water and the bucket of water and object should be the same as the difference of readings on the spring balance between the object in air and in water. Part of the mass of the object is now being carried by the upthrust of the water. However, the volume of the water and object is greater so this is pushing down more on the scales.

Table 10.3

Object	Readings on the scales		Readings on the spring balance	
	weight of bucket	weight of bucket and object	object in air	object in water
stone				

EFFECT OF SALINE SOLUTIONS

Not all liquids have the same upthrust. Objects float better in dense liquids, e.g. oil and salty water. If an egg is placed in fresh water and then salt is added the egg will start to float. Children are usually fascinated by pictures of people floating in the Dead Sea reading newspapers, showing the same type of effect. The difference between salt water and fresh water has to be taken into consideration when loading boats. The children can also relate this to the Plimsoll line, which shows to what level a boat can be loaded depending on what type of seas it will be sailing in (Figure 10.7).

Children can test the density of different liquids. They can make a floater out of a thin stick marked with a $\frac{1}{2}$ cm scale. This floater is then rested upright in different liquids, such as water, salty water, oil and treacle. The floater should float higher in denser liquids.

DISCOVERING THAT PRESSURE INCREASES WITH DEPTH

If the children take old detergent bottles, filled with water, outside and try to find the best way to produce a long jet of water they should discover that the biggest squeeze produces the one that goes furthest. The jets are produced because the water is under pressure. The greater the pressure, or squeeze, the further the jet. The children can then make holes in one of the bottles from the base to the top. While the holes are covered with tape the bottle should

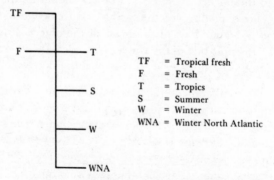

TF = Tropical fresh
F = Fresh
T = Tropics
S = Summer
W = Winter
WNA = Winter North Atlantic

Cold water is denser than warm water so boats float higher. Salt water is denser than fresh water.

Figure 10.7 The Plimsoll line

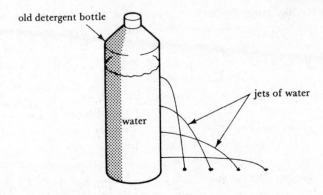

old detergent bottle

jets of water

water

Figure 10.8 Jets of water from a bottle of water

be filled with water. When the children remove the tape they should notice that the lowest hole produces the longest jet of water and the highest the smallest jet (Figure 10.8). Can the children suggest why? The lowest water is being squeezed by the water above and so is under greater pressure.

Resistance in air and water

Some forces resist movement. Children are probably more aware of air resistance than water resistance. The teacher needs to raise this awareness and help the children to clarify and identify it. If the children wave a paper fan, piece of flat cardboard or ceiling tile through the air they should feel how the fan or card has to be pushed against the air and how the air resists. As the children wave the card they should be able feel the difference between holding the card face on or side on to the direction of movement. Once they have recognized the difference they may be able to suggest why. They might test different sizes of card to find that a smaller area moves through the air more easily. The children should hold each card in the same way and aim to wave each card by the same amount.

A simple experiment to relate the pull of gravity and air resistance can be done. Each child needs two postcard-sized cards. The child then stands on a chair, holds the cards flat and drops them simultaneously. The cards should float to the ground and touch at about the same time. The cards are then loaded in different ways by the same number of paper-clips. One card might have eight paper-clips arranged equally around the edges; and the other card might have eight paper-clips on one edge. When the cards are again dropped the children should watch how the cards move through the air and which reaches the ground first.

This experience can be extended by making parachutes. The children should decide how to assess the success of each parachute. They might decide to time the descent from a fixed height or to test the gentleness of landing by measuring the depth of hole left in a sand tray on impact. They might test different materials or different sized canopies. The loads, e.g. cotton reels, must be the same to ensure a fair test. Before testing the children should predict what will happen. This helps them to relate their previous experiments to the new situation. Real parachutes have a small hole at the top of the canopy. The children could test some with holes and some without to see the way they float through the air.

The children could collect pictures of things that are either increasing the effect of air resistance or reducing it. If an object is streamlined it will cut through the air better. A collection of pictures of fast cars will show how they have been designed to reduce the effect of air resistance. Man is not the only species to use the effect of air resistance. Fast-flying birds are streamlined so that the air goes past them easily. Flying foxes have a wide flap of skin between their front limbs and body which enables them to glide through the air. Some seeds, such as those of dandelions, have hairs which act rather like parachutes to help dispersal.

Although children may not have had so much personal experience of moving through water it is easier to demonstrate the effect of water resistance. Many schools have tall containers for measuring capacity. If one ball of plasticine is dropped into one of these containers full of water and another is dropped from the same height in air the children can see the effect of the water on the rate of fall. The children could then time the rate of fall of different shaped pieces of plasticine through water and try to explain why the rates of fall are different. A more streamlined shape will fall faster.

Designs for boats need to take water resistance into account. The children can make a variety of boat shapes and time which move

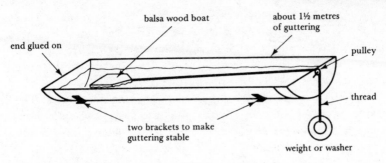

There is no need to have a greater length of guttering than the weight can fall.

Figure 10.9   Investigating how shape affects speed

well through water. Pieces of guttering can be set up as shown in Figure 10.9 to test the boats.

The children cut different shapes out of balsa wood and predict their likely performance. The boats are then timed to find out how fast they travel along the guttering pulled by the dropping weight. Tests could be repeated to ensure the results are valid. The children should test variations of length, width, thickness and roughness of wood to find the factors that make a fast boat and those that make a slow boat.

Friction

If the children have already explored familiar things using energy and forces, such as toys and equipment in the park, in the early years it will be easier to enable them to identify and test situations where friction is significant in the junior classes (Chapter 4).

Friction affects how two surfaces move against each other. The children need a smooth wooden board approximately 20 cm × 10 cm. A hook should be screwed into one end of the wood and an elastic band is placed on the hook (Figure 10.10a). One child slowly pulls the elastic band until the wood starts to move. Another child measures how long the band has to stretch before movement begins. The band initially stretches, rather than pulling the wood, due to the weight of the wood and the friction force. If the children have already been introduced to a force meter they will be able to

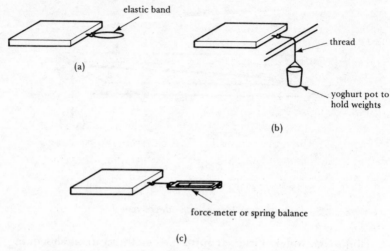

Figure 10.10   Investigating friction

use this as well as an elastic band to measure the force needed to get the wood to move (Figure 10.10b). A third way is to add weights on to a string tied to the hook on the wood until it moves (Figure 10.10c).

The children could try different surfaces, and wood of varying sizes and thickness, to find which move easily. They should make simple hypotheses to explain what they observe. They might say smooth surfaces, small pieces of wood or light pieces of wood allow easier movement because friction is less. They can then try to set up simple experiments to test their hypothesis.

The children may also discover that the force needed to overcome friction and start the block moving is greater than the force needed to keep it going once it is moving. The children can observe how much the elastic band needs to be stretched to get the block to move compared to once the wood has started to move.

Able children can try to find if there is a relationship between the area of the base of wood and force needed to move it. Using a force meter or the method of adding weights will give better results. The children will need to cut wood with different bases, e.g. 10 cm × 5 cm; 10 cm × 10 cm; 10 cm × 15 cm. The wood should be sandpapered so that each piece has the same smoothness. Similarly, other children can try to see if there is a relationship between weight of wood and force needed to overcome friction. The children need to glue sandpaper to a piece of wood and on to the surface it is moved over. They first need to find out what force is needed to move the wood; then a weight is added to the top of the wood. Does the wood now need more force to move it? Is the weight needed to move it the same, more, or less than the weight placed on top of the wood?

It is important that children see the relevance of scientific principles in their everyday life. The children should have discovered that a rough surface causes more friction. They may be able to suggest where this idea is used to help us. For example, they wear trainers with patterned grips for PE. If they are asked to slide a foot on the floor with trainers on and then with just socks on they should notice the difference.

This activity might be taken further. The children could cut out foot shapes from rubber, string, plastic and cloth. The shapes can then be placed on a slope and the angle or height of slope recorded at the point when the foot shape starts to move.

When the brakes are applied on a bicycle friction is at work. In the same way as rough soles on shoes help grip, so does the tread and rubber on the tyres of bicycles and other vehicles. The children could make a collection of rubbings of different tyre patterns. Advice for cyclists, in the form of posters or leaflets, could be produced relating to friction such as 'keep your brakes in good condition'; 'do not use worn tyres'; and 'take care on icy, wet or muddy roads'.

On the other hand some parts of a bicycle need to have the effect of friction reduced as much as possible. Some of the small parts of a bicycle need to be able to move easily against each other. In these cases a lubricant is added. The children could shake hands with a partner and then try to pull their hands away. If they then repeat the activity using first washing-up liquid, then water and finally talcum powder, they should find that the washing-up liquid reduces friction considerably and so makes a good lubricant. In the same way oil is added to the moving parts of a bicycle. However, the children should also be able to appreciate how dangerous it is to get oil or water on the brakes, which is why cyclists and drivers should test their brakes after going through puddles.

There are two other effects of friction. When two things rub together they get hot and often wear each other down. If the children rub their hands together vigorously they should feel them become hot. Prehistoric man applied the idea to start a fire using wood, and friction is still used to light a match by striking it against the side of a rough match-box.

The children will be able to see when they use a rubber to erase something that both the rubber and part of the page is rubbed away. Some children may have clothes with worn areas or holes. They might think of a test to see which materials wear away more quickly than others, perhaps by rubbing different cloths with the same number of rubs with the same pressure on to very coarse sandpaper. Where friction is important for safety on a bicycle, e.g. the brakes and tyres, there need to be regular checks to ensure they have not been worn away to a dangerous state.

A problem-solving activity applying knowledge of forces

At the end of a topic on forces the teacher could provide an open-ended activity to enable the children to apply the knowledge about forces, and to enable assessment of what the children have understood. One such problem is to ask the children to make a device which enables an egg to be dropped from a height of 1 metre or more so that it does not break on reaching the ground.

The children will need to have A4 paper, squares of card approximately 30 cm × 30 cm, string, sticky tape, metre rules, scissors, pencils, rulers, plasticine, staplers and weighing machines provided. They should aim to use as little material as possible. The plasticine should not be used as packing but can be used to make an 'egg' for testing. A real egg is used for the final test. The risk of breaking a real egg adds to the interest and excitement of the activity.

Children who have had experience doing open-ended problems will need very little initial help. They may appreciate the challenge of trying on their own. Other children will need a discussion period before starting to stimulate their thoughts. They might be asked to think how real eggs or Easter eggs are packed to stop them breaking; how delicate parcels are sent through the post; how things are protected when falling, e.g. from an aeroplane; or how a stunt person or commando might get off the top of a high building.

The children are usually extremely imaginative and come up with a variety of solutions. They may invent a slide where friction slows the egg; a parachute or glider using air resistance; a counterbalance system where, as the egg falls, it pulls up a weight that is slightly lighter than it; or they may pack the egg so that the energy of the impact is used by denting the surrounding material rather than cracking the egg.

FURTHER READING

Ardley, N. (1983) *Action Science Working with Water*. London: Franklin Watts.

Bird, J. (1976) *Science from Water Play*. London: Macdonald Educational.

Bryant, J. (1981) *Science Horizons: Floating and Sinking Level 2. West Sussex Science 5-14*. London: Macmillan Educational.

Department of Education and Science and the Welsh Office (1989) *Science in the National Curriculum*. London: HMSO.

Dixon, A. (1983) *Bicycles*. London: A. & C. Black.

Catherall, E. (1983) *Gravity*. Hove: Wayland.

Catherall, E. (1983) *Friction*. Hove: Wayland.

Hodgson, B. and Scanlon, E. (eds) (1985) *Approaching Primary Science*. London: Harper & Row.

Jones, A. (1972) *Structures and Forces*. London: Macdonald Educational/Schools Council.

Kincaid, D. and Coles, P. (1973) *Science in a Topic: Ships*. London: Hulton.

Maun, J. (1982) *Science Horizons: On the Move: Level 1. West Sussex Science 5-14*. London: Macmillan Educational.

Radford, D. (1972) *Science from Toys Stages 1 and 2*. London: Macdonald Educational/Schools Council.

CHAPTER 11
Examining Structures

KEY STAGE 2
During key stage 2 children should study how everyday materials are used in construction and how their properties, such as strength, flexibility and compressibility, influence how they can be used. The children are also expected to explore different forces and use measurements to compare their effects in static structures as well as in moving objects.

During constructional play young children will have developed some appreciation of the limitations and possibilities of different materials and have begun to have a working appreciation of gravity and stability. This empirical knowledge can be extended by practical investigations into building materials and structures. Initially the children might experiment with the properties of wood, concrete and brick to appreciate how they are used in building projects. Further studies of the design of both natural and man-made structures should demonstrate that strength depends on shape and pattern as well as material.

As the children try to make their own structures they can be helped to appreciate how different forces act on these items and the way the forces balance each other in a stable structure.

Investigating building materials

In the early years children will probably have explored the properties of a wide variety of materials through play and simple investigations (Chapter 2). A further study of building materials can extend this work, in the junior years, into considering how the properties of the material influence and limit its use. Originally buildings were made of convenient materials such as stones, clay and wood. As technology improved, better tools and materials enabled people to build more ambitious structures.

Architects and builders need to minimize the amount of material used in a building so that the cost is not too high but they must also ensure high standards of safety. Consequently it is important to know how strong and rigid their materials are. Rigidity is the ability of a structure to withstand being bent, twisted, stretched or changed in shape. Strength is how much force a material can stand before it breaks. Different materials act in different ways when bent or compressed. The children can try bending and squeezing different things, such as chalk, dowelling, thick wire and rubber. They should find that the chalk will snap suddenly but the dowelling will bend initially then splinter and break. The wire will bend but not return to its original position. The rubber bends and returns to its original shape but it may also tear and break. From an activity of this type the children will start to appreciate how important it is that the architect knows how each material will act when a force is applied.

A walk around the school and its environs will enable the children to see where different materials are used. Careful drawings of individual buildings will focus their attention on the ways those materials are applied. The children should find that wood, bricks and concrete are among the most common in use.

WOOD

If wood is to be used in a roof or bridge it is important to know how much weight, e.g. tiles or load of traffic, it can carry before breaking.

Balsa wood is very good for tests in the classroom as the children can cut pieces relatively quickly and easily. The class could be asked to discover the minimum amount of wood needed to make a model bridge across a gap between two tables to carry 100 gm, 500 gm and 1 kg. Different groups of children could test the breaking point of different lengths, widths or thicknesses of wood and report back to the class. One method of testing is to place a strip of wood across the gap between two tables. A bucket is hung on the middle of the strip and the ends are clamped to the tables. Weights are slowly added to the bucket until the wood breaks and the various breaking points can then be recorded and compared. The children should wear goggles to protect their eyes in case the wood jerks upwards and splinters as it breaks. Newspaper placed beneath the bucket will protect the floor. Simple tests of this type can give the children practice in setting up an investigation so that only one variable is changed at a time to ensure the test is fair. The tests can be extended by investigating whether strength varies when the wood is wet.

As the children test the breaking points of wood they should notice that it bends before breaking. When manufacturing some things, such as boats or tennis rackets, this property is an asset, but building structures need to be rigid. Tests can be performed to discover how different types of wood, and different thicknesses, lengths and widths, alter with increasing loads. These experiments could be set up as shown in Figure 11.1.

It is important that only one variable is changed during each test. One group of children could test how much different types of wood bend under 100 gm, 200 gm, 300 gm, etc. In this case only the

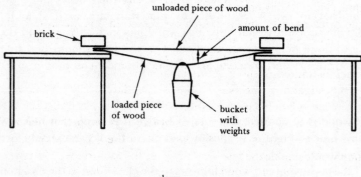

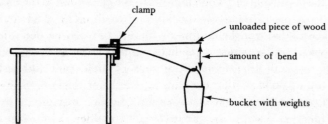

Figure 11.1 Methods of investigating bend in wood

wood type changes; the length, width and thickness must be kept the same.

Builders need to consider how the materials will be influenced by different weather conditions. The children may have already noticed that wooden toys are damaged when left out in the rain. If they draw round and weigh a piece of wood before and after it has been soaked they should find that it expands and becomes heavier. If the children look at how wood is treated in existing buildings, they may be able to suggest how these undesirable changes can be minimized. They could then treat their own samples with different substances, such as water-based paints, gloss paint, varnish and glue, to see which are effective in keeping out water.

BRICKS

A collection of bricks can lead the children to look for differences in colour, shape, cavities, texture, lettering, weight and size. The children can be asked to suggest why most bricks are the same size and shape. If they have seen a bricklayer at work, they can see that the brick must be small enough to be held in one hand while the bricklayer applies the mortar with the other. Therefore, although it is quicker to complete a building with large bricks, the size of the brick is limited to the size and weight easily lifted in one hand.

Investigations into which shapes tessellate easily will demonstrate the advantages of cuboids and cubes for building. Initially the children may feel that a cube would be more convenient as it does not matter which face is placed on to the wall. This observation would enable the teacher to suggest the importance of strength as well as speed of construction. When the children look closely at the construction of a brick wall they will see that the bricks overlap. The teacher could ask them to design and carry out a test to compare the strength of a wall made of overlapping toy bricks with one made of bricks that do not overlap. To ensure the test is fair it is important to apply the same force to each wall in the same way. The children may decide to set up a device that swings or rolls increasing weights against the walls and then count how many bricks have been dislodged. The common brick patterns or bonds could be compared in the same way (Figure 11.2). This experience should enable the children to appreciate the advantage of a cuboid shape for bricks, as it is easier to overlap them to give a strong structure.

Although bricks are a common size, they vary quite considerably in weight, blue engineering bricks being particularly heavy. Some children may suggest that the variation between two bricks is due to there being less material because of the cavity or frog, others that the actual material is heavier. They can discover which is correct by finding the weight per cubic centimetre and comparing the results for each brick. This can be calculated by finding the volume of the brick, by displacement of water, and dividing this figure by the weight of the brick.

When some bricks are placed in water the children may notice air bubbles rising, indicating that the brick is porous. The children can find out how much water can be absorbed by each brick by weighing them when dry and then after being left in water for a few hours. Some bricks, like the blue engineering brick, are not porous because the material is dense, but as these are expensive the architect must find a way of using the cheaper bricks so that the house does not become damp after rain. This is usually achieved by using a dampcourse and cavity wall. Simple activities to show how these methods work can be set up as shown in Figure 11.3.

As coloured water is added to the first dish, the bottom cubes become coloured but the plastic 'dampcourse' stops the upward movement (until the cubes collapse). By using two materials with different properties in this way the builder can combine the advantages of strength of the bricks with the waterproof plastic to reduce the disadvantages of the brick's porosity. In the second activity the children can see that the outer wall becomes damp and coloured by the 'rain' but acts as a protective barrier for the inside wall which remains dry.

CONCRETE

Unlike wood and bricks, wet concrete can be poured into moulds of almost any shape and size. The children can easily make different mixtures of concrete and pour them into their own moulds. Yoghurt pots could be used as moulds or more standard concrete rods can be made for tests using wooden moulds (Figure 11.4).

Wall made without bricks overlapping

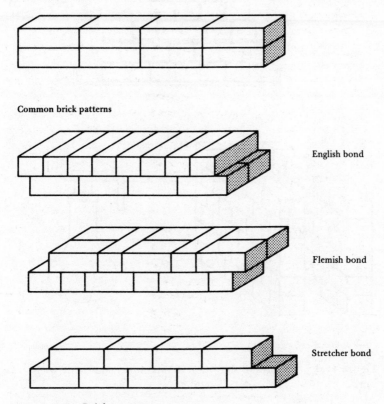

Common brick patterns

English bond

Flemish bond

Stretcher bond

Figure 11.2 Brick patterns

Vaseline should be wiped around the inside of the mould so that the concrete can be removed once it has set. Different groups could mix up different proportions of cement, sand and gravel. Different proportions of cement, sand and gravel are commonly used for different purposes. Foundations often have proportions of 1:3:5; floors and beams have proportions of 1:2:4; and roofs are made with proportions of 1:2:3. One of the children's mixtures could be made of one cup of cement, one cup of sand and one cup of gravel. Another mixture might be one cup of cement, two of sand and one of gravel. Water is added until the mixture has the consistency of mashed potato. After two or three days the bars can be removed

181

A dampcourse

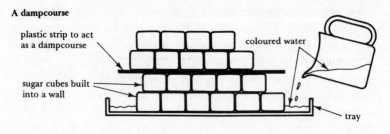

plastic strip to act
as a dampcourse

coloured water

sugar cubes built
into a wall

tray

A cavity wall

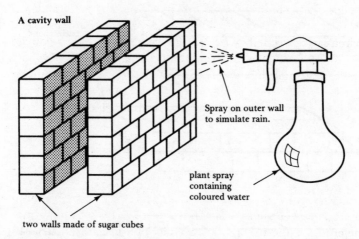

Spray on outer wall
to simulate rain.

plant spray
containing
coloured water

two walls made of sugar cubes

Figure 11.3 Activities to show how dampcourses and cavity walls
work

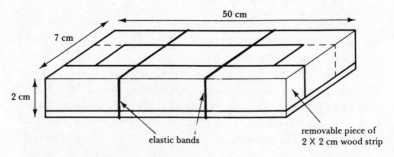

50 cm

7 cm

2 cm

elastic bands

removable piece of
2 X 2 cm wood strip

Figure 11.4 Mould for making concrete

from the moulds and tested, in the same way as the wooden strips, to find the breaking points. The children will find that quite large loads of about 5 kg will be needed. They will also discover that, unlike wood, concrete becomes stronger with time. After a few days it will be very difficult to break most of the bars at all.

When concrete is compressed or squeezed it is very strong but it is weaker when stretched or bent. Children can see the differences between forces of tension and compression when they bend a rubber (Figure 11.5).

Builders often limit this weakness in concrete by re-inforcing it with metal rods, as wire bends and does not easily crack. The children can make their own reinforced concrete by adding florists' wire to some of their concrete bars and comparing them with bars made of the same mixture without wire. Again by combining materials with different properties, builders can exploit the advantageous properties of the materials and minimize their limitations.

Ways of using shape to strengthen structures

INVESTIGATING RIGIDITY IN SHAPE

During the study of brick bonds the children will have begun to appreciate that shape as well as the type of material is important in determining the strength and rigidity of a structure. They can explore this further by making shapes with strips of card held together with paper fasteners to discover which are rigid. Initially the teacher could suggest some shapes and ask the children to predict whether they will be rigid when pushed gently on one side (Figure 11.6).

After their predictions the children can make the shapes and test

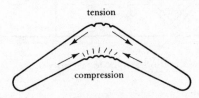

tension

compression

Figure 11.5 Forces of tension and compression in a bent rubber

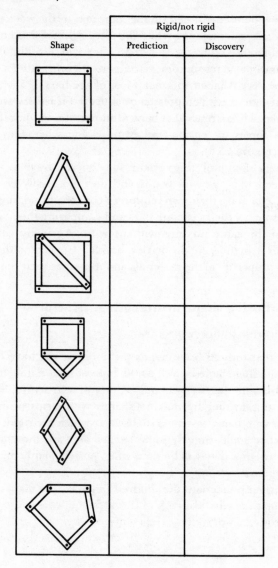

Figure 11.6 Investigating shapes for rigidity

them and try to identify the feature common to all the rigid ones. Their ideas can be tested by making their own rigid structure or adding strips to make the non-rigid shapes firm. The children should find that a framework made of triangles cannot be pulled or pushed out of shape. A variety of 3D shapes could also be made with straws fixed with short pipe cleaners or folded strips of card to discover that the triangle is as important in these constructions.

STRENGTHENING MATERIALS BY FOLDING OR BENDING

A horizontal piece of card will resist bending if its opposite sides are pushed together horizontally. Once the card starts to bend it will buckle up or downwards. If the card is folded at right angles along its length the resultant piece can no longer bend easily up or down so has strength in all directions. This principle is just as applicable whether the structure is made of steel, concrete or paper. By investigating paper structures the children can discover how materials can be strengthened by bending or folding them.

Open-ended problems can start the children thinking about ways of strengthening materials. They could be asked to use glue and only one piece of A4 paper to make a bridge that will span a gap of 20 cm between two blocks and carry a weight of 100 gm. Multibase blocks and bricks make good supports. This can be achieved by cutting the paper into two or three long strips and making tubes or folding the paper into a concertina. Another activity is to ask the children again to use only one piece of A4 paper and a square piece of card to make as tall a tower as possible that can support 1 kg. There are several solutions which involve folding or rolling the paper, including making a tube shape with the card resting on top to spread the weight.

It is important that the children understand that failure of their structure gives information. If they notice where the structure has bent, buckled, stretched or twisted they can try to fold the paper to resist this movement. Robert Johnsey's book *Problem Solving in School Science* has several extension ideas to investigate paper structures further.

After opportunities to invent ways of strengthening paper the children could analyse and measure the comparative effectiveness of different methods. This can be done by making bridges out of

Bridge design	Weight needed to make bridge sag	Comments
one sheet of card		
two sheets of card glued together		
three sheets of card glued together		
 card folded into a W-girder		
 W-girder and a sheet of card glued together		
 H-girder and a sheet of card glued together		
 two struts beneath bridge		
 arch		
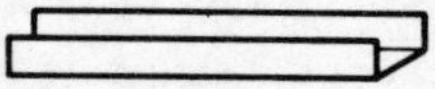 two vertical 'joists'		
own invention		

Figure 11.7   Investigating ways of strengthening paper

card to span a width of 15 cm between two blocks of equal height. The card should be about 4 cm by 20 cm. Weights are added to each structure until the bridge sags and the results recorded in a table like the one shown in Figure 11.7.

A tube provides a stronger structure than a flat piece of paper as it resists twisting and bending in any direction. Bundles of tubes are even stronger. The children can be given 20 straws and asked to tape them to make a flat bridge and then test what weight the bridge will take before sagging. Another 20 tubes can be grouped into two or three bundles tied with elastic bands and tested in the same way. The children will find these have even greater strength (Figure 11.8).

Pillars are often made of tube-like structures. Children can test different shaped tubes with square, circular, triangular and hexagonal cross-sections by placing weights on top of them until they collapse. The weights should be placed in the centre of a card resting on the top of each pillar to spread the weight evenly. Each pillar should be made of the same thickness and size of card to ensure the test is fair. A similar investigation can consider the

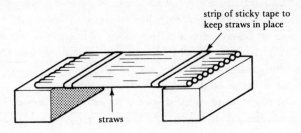

strip of sticky tape to keep straws in place

straws

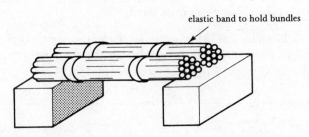

elastic band to hold bundles

Figure 11.8   Increasing strength by bundling tubes together

comparative strength of different diameters or heights of pillar. This type of activity helps children to appreciate the need to change only one variable in a fair test. For example, if the comparative strength of different heights is being examined the diameters and shapes must remain the same. Different groups of children could carry out different experiments and report their results to the whole class.

Tubes are a common form of structure that combines reduced weight and strength and they are found in the natural world as well as in manufactured goods. The long arm and leg bones in the human skeleton are hollow so that they are both light and strong. Trees and other plants have many tubes in their trunks and stems which not only carry food and water but also give strength. Hexagonal honeycombs have the similar strength of bundles of tubes and as hexagons tessellate they have the additional strength of a close fit.

There are many examples of stiffening of materials in the school and environs. It is common to see steel girders folded into right angles. Bicycle frames use tubing to make the machine light but strong. Plastic chairs often have their edges curved over; plastic buckets and tidy boxes frequently have the rim or edges thickened, turned over or folded into a girder shape. Thin plastic food and drinks cartons use systems of folds or curves in the material to give strength. Full skirts use similar techniques by having a narrow rolled hem or fabric gathered or folded in layers.

A study of bridges is an ideal way of investigating how different forces are balanced or taken into account to give a safe stable structure.

Investigating the design of bridges

If the children look at bridges around the school area and pictures of bridges they may be able to identify the four main types of bridge: beam, arch, suspension and cantilever.

BEAM BRIDGES

A beam bridge is basically a plank across a span. Many of the previous experiments have involved activities testing the strength or rigidity of materials using this type of construction.

If the children roll some soft plasticine into a long snake shape and place it across the span between two blocks it will sag in the middle. This demonstrates that objects have body weight and bend due to the force of gravity under their own weight (Figure 11.9a). If a load is added it will sag even further. From their previous experiments the children will realize that too great a load will cause structural failure and the beam will break. There are several ways of overcoming this sag: reinforcing the material as in reinforced concrete, using additional supports, bending up the sides of the bridge in the same way that folding paper at right angles gave strength, building an arch underneath the beam or by suspending the beam on cables.

The children can test the effect of adding supports by first finding out how much weight a bridge made of a long strip of card can hold before collapsing, compared to one made of the same amount of card with 1, 2, 3 . . . supports (Figure 11.9b). Although adding supports increases the carrying capacity of the bridge they may be so close that cars or boats can not pass between them.

Another solution is to limit the bend of the beam by building up the sides. The children can test the effect of folding the side of the card as shown in Figure 11.9c. If they note carefully where the paper starts to bend they can try bracing these places and then test to see if this structure is stronger (Figure 11.9d).

To have the same strengthening effect the sides of the beam need not be made of the same material. They could be made of a lighter material and constructed in a lattice framework to reduce the basic body weight. This lattice is very likely to be based on triangle shapes, which the children will have already discovered give a rigid structure. The children could make different lattices to test their strengths. As the builder must consider economy as well as strength they could record the number of strips of card needed as well as the weight carried before sagging or breaking occurs (Figure 11.9e).

ARCH BRIDGES

An arch is another method used to stop the downward bend of a flat beam. The children can discover this by comparing the weight

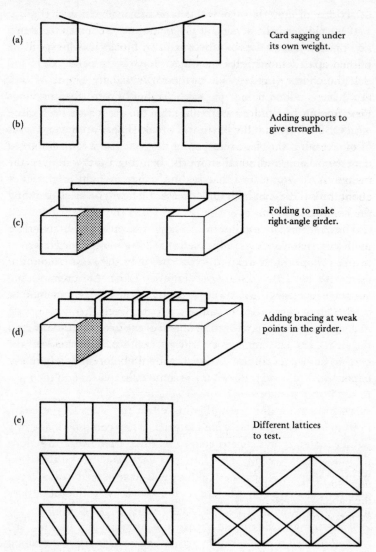

(a) Card sagging under its own weight.

(b) Adding supports to give strength.

(c) Folding to make right-angle girder.

(d) Adding bracing at weak points in the girder.

(e) Different lattices to test.

Figure 11.9 Beam bridges

a flat beam of card can carry with one supported by an arch (Figure 11.10a). The weight of the load is spread by the arch to the two side bricks. If light blocks are used instead of bricks they will be pushed apart, showing the need for very solid supports.

If the children make their own arch with polystyrene or clay bricks they will be helped to see the importance of the keystone. First they should draw around the base of a tin or jar on a piece of card. They should then draw the wedge-shaped stones as shown in Figure 11.10b. The central stone or keystone is usually larger than the others. These shapes are cut out and used as templates for the polystyrene or clay. If polystyrene tiles are used a thickness of about three tiles is necessary. Once the clay has dried and hardened the arch can be built over the tin, which is then gently removed (Figure 11.10c). The children will find that without the last piece in the centre the arch will collapse. As the keystone is pulled downwards under its own weight by the force of gravity it is fixed more firmly into its space thus making the structure more secure.

Arches are fairly common in natural objects, e.g. snails and eggs. The strength of eggs can be demonstrated by collecting egg shells and cutting them to make four halves which are then placed arch upwards with a piece of hardboard on top. The children will see that this structure can hold several books before the eggs finally break.

SUSPENSION BRIDGES

In suspension bridges cables are used to hold up the beam. If the children try to build a model suspension bridge, perhaps using a picture of an existing one for guidance, they will soon find when they add loads to the model that they need to anchor the ends of the cables to stop the towers leaning inwards. The children could then try to identify all the forces acting in the model. The weight of the load or traffic going over the bridge is downwards. This is balanced by the upward action of the cables. The pull inwards by the cables on the towers is counteracted by the cables to the anchors. The towers are pushed down by the weight and action of the cables. This is balanced by the force of the ground pushing upwards against the base of the towers. Unless these forces are balanced there will be movement and the bridge will collapse.

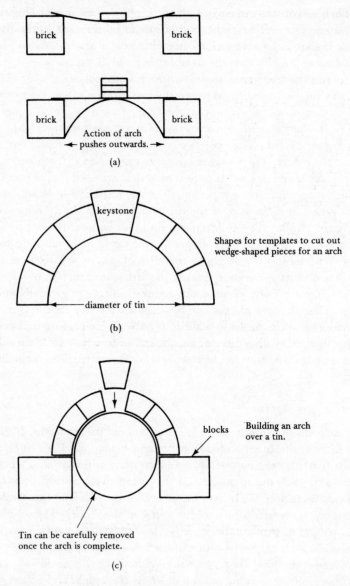

brick · brick

brick · brick

Action of arch
◄— pushes outwards. —►

(a)

keystone

Shapes for templates to cut out
wedge-shaped pieces for an arch

—diameter of tin—

(b)

blocks · Building an arch
over a tin.

Tin can be carefully removed
once the arch is complete.

(c)

Figure 11.10 Comparing the load that can be carried by a piece of
card with and without an arch

Symmetry plays an important part in the overall strength of any construction as it is easier to balance all the component forces when the structure is symmetrical.

CANTILEVER BRIDGES

The cantilever bridge has a complicated set of forces in balance. Initially the children could be asked to build a diving platform so that it extends as far as possible beyond a tower with a 100-gm weight on the end. They should only use a block for the tower, a thick piece of card or wood and other weights. They will find that they need to place weights on the card resting on the tower to balance the 100-gm weight (Figure 11.11a). A crane is designed as a type of cantilever and like the diving board needs a counterbalance to offset the load it is lifting.

The two sides of a cantilever bridge are constructed in a similar

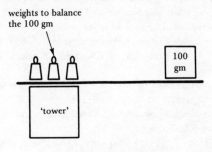

(a) Building a diving platform.

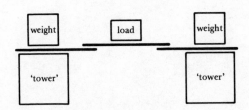

(b) Investigating the weights needed to balance a cantilever bridge.

Figure 11.11 Cantilever structures

way (Figure 11.11b). The children could experiment with different weights at the towers and centre and with different positions of the towers in order to design a model bridge using the minimum amount of card and weight that can carry a toy truck loaded with a 100-gm weight as it is pushed across.

A project on bridges could include studies of famous bridges and their builders and notable disasters and why they happened. A final open-ended problem such as building a bridge to span two metres between desks using only newspaper, sticky tape and string would enable the children to apply the ideas they have learnt and allow the teacher to assess whether the children have understood the concepts.

FURTHER READING

Bull, R. (1989) *Starting Design and Technology: Structures*. London: Cassell.

Department of Education and Science and the Welsh Office (1989) *Science in the National Curriculum*. London: HMSO.

Dixon, A. (1981) *Science Explorers: Bridges*. London: A.& C.Black.

Jennings, T. (1984) *The Young Scientist Investigates: Structures*. Oxford: Oxford University Press.

Johnsey, R. (1986) *Problem Solving in School Science*. Hemel Hempstead: Macdonald Educational.

James, A. (1972) *Structures and Forces: Stages 1 and 2*. London: Macdonald Educational/Schools Council.

Kincaid, D. and Coles P. (1979) *Science in a Topic: Roads, Bridges and Tunnels*. London: Hulton.

CHAPTER 12
Models and Machines

KEY STAGE 2

During the junior years children are expected to learn that models and machines need a source of energy in order to work, and that this energy can be stored and transferred to and from moving things. These concepts can be presented to the children by studying existing machines and by making models. Alongside this work ideas relating to forces which involve movement can be incorporated.

Defining and classifying machines

Many children do not have a clear idea how to explain what a machine is. In order to discover what ideas they already have, the teacher could give the children several old magazines and ask them to collect pictures of machines. This collection will give an impression of the children's views which can be used to ask them to try to define or explain what a machine is. Children tend to choose complicated systems, such as aeroplanes, washing machines, tanks and computers and suggest definitions like: machines run on electricity, they are made of moving parts, or they need a fuel. Once the children have started to clarify their ideas they may wish to add other items to their collection that match with their explanation but are not normally thought of as machines by children, such as watches, wheelbarrows and food whisks.

Having started from the children's own ideas and understanding the teacher can build on or question these ideas in order to help the children to understand that a machine enables us to move or do something more easily or quickly in one or more of these ways:

- It can move energy from one place to another. A hand whisk moves energy supplied by the hand to the beaters.

- A machine can also magnify energy. By using a series of cogs one turn of the handle on the whisk moves the beaters through several rotations.
- The machine may also change energy from one sort into another; for example, a generator changes moving energy into electrical energy.

All machines need a source of energy in order to work. This may be energy provided by muscles or by electricity, oil, petrol, coal, etc. So the children who suggest that a fuel is needed are close to a partial explanation.

Once the children have a clearer idea of what a machine is, they can add to their pictures from magazines and then suggest ways of classifying them. Different groups could try different classifications and discuss which are most appropriate. They may choose sets of transport types, machines with and without wheels or sets related to location, e.g. found in the home, school or factory. If one group sorts out sets related to different energy sources, it should be possible to include all the machines in one or more of the sets, reinforcing the idea that all machines need an energy source. The cut-out pictures of machines could be used to record different classifications or to make collages, perhaps in-filling shapes of different machines.

There are several basic types of movement and mechanisms to be found in machines. The most common mechanisms are levers, pulleys, belts, gears, cams, screws and ratchets. To develop the work further the teacher could either investigate one machine in detail or ask the children to study several household machines. As most of the concepts and vocabulary will be new to the children it seems better to study one machine in detail to provide a secure foundation so that the children can have the confidence of recognizing some features when they explore new machines. Readily available actual examples of the machine chosen for close study are ideal. A trip to a building site could initiate an in-depth study of cranes, or a bicycle brought into the classroom could fire the children's enthusiasm to study bicycles.

Cranes

Science and technology could be closely linked by setting the children a challenge that they should make a working model of a crane. The planning could include studying real cranes and pictures to identify the various components of the crane. The children should be able to identify the cab, wheels, winch, cable and end-tackle. Different groups could then perform simple tests to advise the others on appropriate materials and designs for making the various parts.

One group could test different materials for use as a cable. They might choose to test wool, cotton and pipe cleaners. The children should try to work out a fair test for assessing the strength of the different materials. One method is to fix a yoghurt pot on to each 'cable', hang it over the edge of a table and load the pot with weights until breaking point. If pipe cleaners are used the children usually predict they will be the strongest because they are made of wire. However, they usually break quickly at the joins, demonstrating to the children that the method of joining materials is very important and that the strength of a device is related to the weakest point. The children could also test the comparative strength of cables made of one, two or three pieces of cotton.

Another group could prepare a report on possible end-tackles. This group could be given a variety of items to pick up with their hands, such as marbles, pins, metal washers, footballs and cloths. If the children look very carefully at how their hands pick up each of these items, they can design an appropriate device. Some things need a pinching device, others a scoop and others can be picked up easily with a magnet.

Yet another group could design a pulley and winch. This group need to have the same type of cable for each test. Initially they could be given a piece of wood with sharp edges and a piece of rounded dowel and be asked to observe what weight the cable can hold before breaking, if it is jerked upwards compared with being pulled up slowly and steadily; and how much force, using a force meter (designed like a spring balance), is needed to raise the same weight over the square wood compared to the dowelling (Figure 12.1a).

The children should find that if a cotton cable is jerked upwards it is more likely to break than if it is lifted with a steady pull. It also

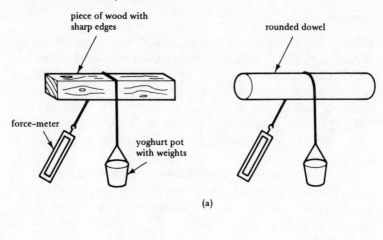

piece of wood with sharp edges

rounded dowel

force-meter

yoghurt pot with weights

(a)

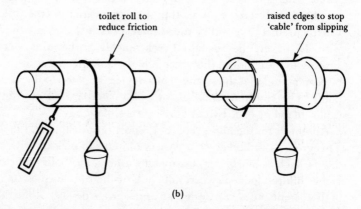

toilet roll to reduce friction

raised edges to stop 'cable' from slipping

(b)

Figure 12.1 Steps to discover the reasons behind the design of a pulley

requires less force to lift the weight over the rounded surface because there is less friction. When the children look at the real crane, they should see that this is solved by the cable being pulled on a series of wheels. If they add a toilet roll (Figure 12.1b) even less force will be needed to pull the weight upwards. However, the cotton is likely to slip off the edge of the roll unless raised edges are added. This process of development demonstrates to the children why a pulley is a wheel with a groove for the rope or cable.

As the children pull the cable to raise the weight, they should discover the need to wind up the spare cotton on a wheel or winch

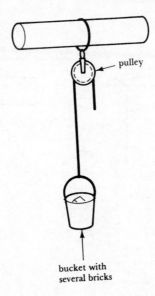

pulley

bucket with
several bricks

Figure 12.2   A pulley

with a turning mechanism to ensure that the cotton does not become tangled and can be pulled up or lowered steadily without jerking. Further work on pulleys can follow. A single pulley could be set up using netball posts or a convenient roof beam (Figure 12.2).

The children will find it is much easier to lift the bucket using the pulley system than by themselves. With some prompting the children should realize that when they try to lift the bucket by themselves they are having to lift against the force of gravity, whereas when they pull down on the rope which goes through the pulley they are using gravity to help them. Two or more pulleys could be set up for the children to discover that it is now even easier to lift the bucket but the rate of movement upwards is smaller.

Once the investigations are complete the children could design and make the crane. One possible design is shown in Figure 12.3.

Bicycles

A topic on bicycles enables wheels, cogs and gears to be studied in detail with reference to an actual machine. The activities could also

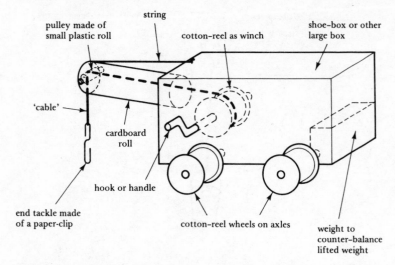

Figure 12.3 Design for a crane

include considering friction and lubrication (see Chapter 10); why different materials are used for different parts; and work on lights using batteries and generators. A study of the historical development of the bicycle can show how the technological improvements of lighter and more comfortable materials, brakes and gears were related to consumer demands of increased safety, comfort, speed, etc.

The teacher may wish to start by recapping previous work already carried out on wheels (Chapter 4). It is usually fairly easy to arrange for an actual bicycle to be brought into the classroom so that the children can study it in detail, to locate all the types of wheels and try to explain how each is turned. The system of the pedal, chain wheel and rear wheel is an excellent example of a device that transfers energy. If the children look carefully they will see that the chain wheel and rear wheel turn in the same direction. The chain wheel has teeth to reduce slipping.

Simple devices made of cotton-reels and elastic bands can extend the idea of transferred energy and how the positioning of the band affects the direction of turn (Figure 12.4). The children should first predict the direction of turn of the unmarked cotton-reels and then try them out.

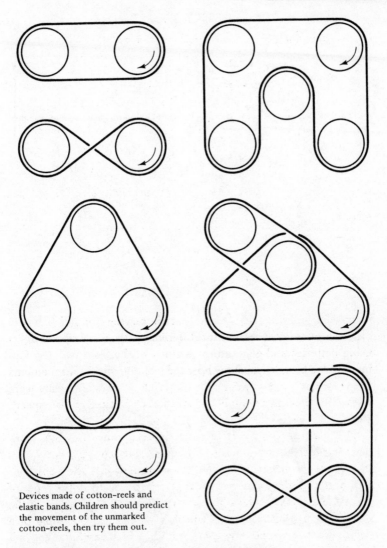

Devices made of cotton-reels and
elastic bands. Children should predict
the movement of the unmarked
cotton-reels, then try them out.

Figure 12.4 Investigating belts which transfer energy

A band is unnecessary if the wheels have teeth and are adjoining.
The children can make a set of moving gear wheels out of serrated
bottle tops by hammering the tops on to a piece of wood so that
as one turns another will move. The children will soon find out that
it is very important to place the nail in the centre of the top. It is

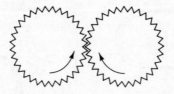

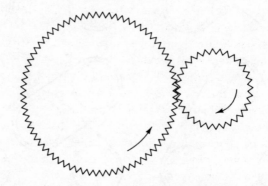

(a) An anticlockwise movement of one wheel creates a clockwise movement of the other.

(b) The small wheel will turn round twice for each complete turn of the large wheel.

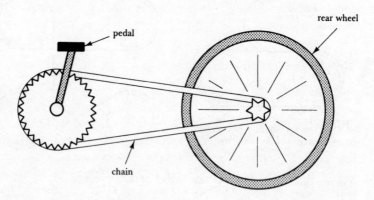

(c) Cogs and chain system of a bicycle

Figure 12.5 Investigating the movement of cogs

quite difficult to position more than four tops so that they all move. If the children look at the relative movement of the tops they should find that if one is turning anticlockwise the adjoining one will turn clockwise (Figure 12.5a).

Constructional materials, such as Technical Lego, enable the children to study the effect of using gear wheels of different sizes.

If both wheels are marked the children will find that they only need to turn the large wheel once to make the small one turn several times (Figure 12.5b), demonstrating one way a machine magnifies effort. A bicycle gear, food whisk and hand drill all use this principle. If the children look at the actual bicycle, they will see that the pedal drives the chain which turns a small wheel. This small wheel turns several times for each turn of the pedal. As this small wheel is fixed to the rear wheel, the latter turns at the same rate as the small wheel (Figure 12.5c). The cyclist provides the energy to turn the pedals. The children can see that the 'machine' magnifies this effort as every time the pedal turns once the rear wheel turns several times. On old bicycles, such as the penny-farthing, the pedal was fixed to the centre of the wheel, so for every turn of the pedal the bicycle went forward only the distance of one circumference of the wheel. The very large wheel on the Penny Farthing maximized the distance travelled for each turn of the pedal. This rather dangerous design was unnecessary once the idea of gears was used.

Simple household machines

Once the children have the foundation of some aspects of one machine they have probably enough experience to look at a variety of other machines to see how they work, sort them and identify and investigate other mechanical features. Items such as a bottle opener, ice cream scoop, hand mixer, hand drill, old clocks, scissors, nutcracker, spade, claw hammer, wheelbarrow and tweezers give a variety of types of machines. Initially the children could be given the machines to discuss and try to work out how they work. If unusual items can be included, that the children do not recognize, this makes an added challenge.

The children could also be given several tasks which they have to attempt first using their fingers and then with a machine. These tasks could include removing a tightly fitting lid from a tin, halving a piece of cloth and breaking open a nut. This type of activity will help the children to understand that even devices like the screwdriver, which have no moving parts, are machines because they enable us to move something more easily or quickly. Once the children have had an opportunity to study the machines in detail they could sort them into the main types of mechanism: levers, pulleys, gears, screws and ratchets. They could also try to identify the four types of movement: a straight line in one direction, reciprocal (backward and forwards), rotary (circular) and oscillating (backwards and forwards in an arc) (Figure 12.6).

The screw is based on the principle that it is easier to move a weight up a slope than by lifting it. The children can appreciate this if they are given a heavy bag of sand and asked to test whether it is easier to lift it directly on to a table or to drag it up a plank of wood. In the same way a winding road up a mountain is easier than a direct route. A screw is like a small winding slope.

Children find levers rather complicated because there are three types. Initially they can be challenged to find a way of lifting a brick off the ground with only one finger, using a piece of dowel and a plank of wood. This can be done if the dowel is placed beneath the plank near the brick as shown in Figure 12.7a. The dowelling acts as a fulcrum. The relationship between the load and the force or effort needed can be explored by using a ruler, dowelling and weights. If the children move the dowelling as shown in Figure 12.7b they should find out what weights are needed to balance a fixed weight of 100 gm. They should discover that if the fulcrum is near the fixed weight fewer weights, or less effort, are needed to balance it. Able children could try the effect of moving the weights and keeping the fulcrum fixed in the centre of the ruler. They should discover that when the distance from the fulcrum is doubled the weight needed to make a balance is halved (Figure 12.7c).

The more able children can try to identify different types of lever. In these the fulcrum is not in the centre of the machine. A nutcracker and a wheelbarrow have the fulcrum at one end with the load in the centre. A spade is an example of the third type. When the gardener is lifting a load of earth the handle is acting as a fulcrum and the effort is in the centre of the spade (Figure 12.8).

Gears

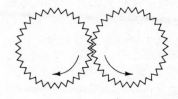

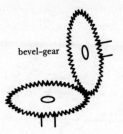

bevel-gear

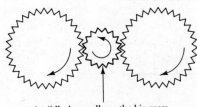

An 'idler' gear allows the big gears to turn in the same direction.

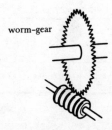

worm-gear

Bevel-gears and worm-gears enable energy to be transferred from a horizontal axis to a vertical axis or vice versa.

Ratchet

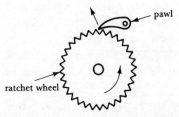

pawl

ratchet wheel

The pawl stops the wheel slipping backwards.

Screw

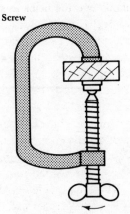

When the nut is turned the screw moves upwards.

Figure 12.6 Simple machines

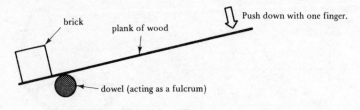

(a) Lifting a brick with one finger.

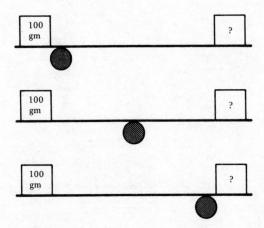

(b) Investigating the effect of moving the fulcrum.

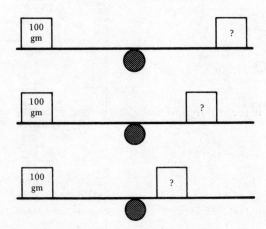

(c) Investigating the effect of moving the effort (or push down).

Figure 12.7 Levers

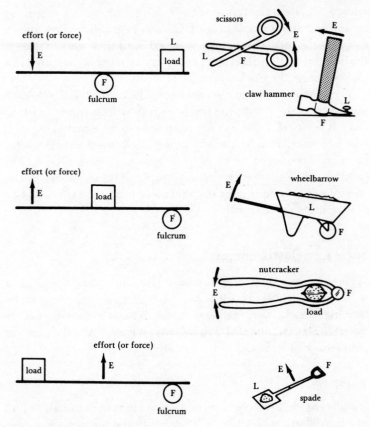

Figure 12.8 Types of lever

Constructional kits, such as Technical Lego, have guided activities which enable the children to make many types of machines.

Stored or potential energy

Stored, or potential, energy means that although the energy is not at that moment making anything happen, it could do so. When a book is put on a high shelf energy is used to lift it against the force of gravity. As long as the book stays where it is put it has a form of stored energy known as height energy or 'gravitational potential energy'. If the book tips off the shelf it will fall using its stored energy. Children can try using their own energy to pick something up and place it on a table or shelf. Climbing up a slide needs energy to get to the top. This energy is stored until they start to slide to the bottom. As they slide down, the stored energy is converted into movement or 'kinetic' energy.

The increase in height does not have to be vertical. If the children push a truck up a slope the height energy will be stored until the truck is released. Machines are often used to raise materials, all of which need energy. The model crane might need muscle energy or energy produced by an electric motor to raise a load. The children will find that in every example of lifting, some sort of energy will be used to raise the load away from the earth's surface to give it height energy.

Spring or elastic energy

Spring or elastic energy can also be stored. This can be done in four ways: by stretching; by squeezing, squashing or compression; by bending; and by twisting. Once these materials are released the stored energy is converted into movement energy and the material jumps back or untwists.

ELASTICITY

Initially the children could sort different kinds of materials to find which are elastic or flexible, i.e. bend easily and spring back to their original shape. The children's findings could be recorded into the categories shown in Table 12.1.

Table 12.1

Rigid, does not bend easily	Plastic, bends easily but does not spring back	Flexible, bends easily and springs back to its original shape
sponge bandage clay		

The flexible materials will be able to store energy. Rubber bands are easily available and enable the children to explore elasticity. Many packets of elastic bands contain bands of different length and thickness. Different groups could be given several investigations.

- Does one long band stretch more than one short band?
- Do thick bands stretch more or less than thin bands?
- Which is the stronger, a thick or thin rubber band?
- Do rubber bands stretch by a regular or irregular amount when 100 gm, 200 gm, 300 gm, etc. is hung on the end of the band?

Questions of this type involve the children designing and performing fair tests: identifying the variable that they are investigating, ensuring all the other variables are kept the same, and carrying out each test in the same way. In the first example the only variable that can change is the length. The two bands must have the same width and the same weight needs to be hung on the bottom of each band. The difference in stretch can then be measured.

One way to find the stronger band between a thick and thin band is to fix a bucket to each of the bands and add weights steadily until breaking point. The children are likely to be surprised to find that the bands will be able to take several kilograms before breaking. For safety reasons children near the experiment should wear goggles in case the bands break suddenly and spring into their eyes. The floor under the weights should be cushioned with newspapers to stop damage when they fall.

When the children try the final activity they should discover that elastic bands stretch at a steady amount when increasing weights are added. This property enables bands to be used to make simple weighing machines. The children need string, a yoghurt pot or beaker, Sellotape, about eight rubber bands, a long strip of paper, a 100-gram weight and a drawing pin. The bands should be looped together. A handle should be fixed on to the beaker and attached to the line of bands. The equipment is then set up as shown in Figure 12.9a.

While the beaker is empty, a line should be drawn on the strip of paper level with the top of the beaker. It is important that the children look with their eye level with the top of the pot. Then 100 grams is put in the beaker and a new line drawn to mark the new

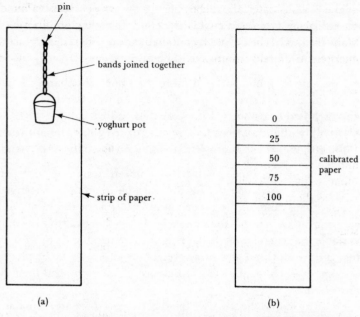

Figure 12.9 Making a simple weighing machine with elastic bands

position of the beaker. The strip can then be removed from the wall, folded half way between the two marks, and folded again to make quarters. These marks should be calibrated as shown in Figure 12.9b. When the paper is returned to its original position on the wall the children can test out the accuracy of their machine by weighing different items, such as pencils, scissors and rubbers, with their own weighing machine and a school balance. By making a weighing machine of this type the children should be able to understand how a spring balance works. The weight pulls on the machine and stretches the elastic or spring. The amount of stretch depends on the weight. Energy is stored in the spring or elastic until the weight is removed and then the elastic or spring jumps back to its original shape.

Rubber bands can also store energy by being twisted. When the band is released the stored energy is converted to movement energy as the band untwists. The children could be asked to make a model using elastic power. There are many possibilities: a cart, round-about, a spider which bounces on an elastic thread, paddle boat or vehicle with a propeller using twisted bands, or a catapult to launch an aeroplane or missile (see Chapter 4). Once the children have made the model they could be asked to explain how it works, what energy is used and whether it is stored.

BOUNCING BALLS

Investigating the action of balls enables the children to compare the elasticity of different materials in a familiar context. Some materials, such as plasticine, absorb the energy when they are squeezed and have no spring back, some are too rigid to be compressed but other solid materials are very elastic. Air inside some objects enables them to be springy. When the object is squashed the air is compressed and on being released it springs back to its original shape.

The children could be asked to find the best bouncer from a collection of balls of varying sizes and materials, including airflow, sponge, tennis, golf and small beach balls, marbles and ball bearings. If the children are given an open-ended problem of this type they will have the opportunity to carry out a complete investigation for themselves. Initially they need to identify the variable that will alter and keep all the others unchanged. There is likely to be considerable discussion both before and during the activity about ensuring fairness.

If the children throw the ball into the air, they need to ensure each ball is thrown with the same force. If the balls land on different places they may bounce differently. There is also the problem of how to register how high the ball bounces. The children will probably need time to review and improve their experimental procedure.

One method of testing the balls is to drop them from a fixed height, such as 1 metre, on to the same surface. If the balls are dropped close to a wall, a piece of paper can be fixed to the wall so that the position of the top of the bounce can be quickly marked. One child drops, not throws, the ball while another observes the point of highest bounce. The children will find that the height of bounce varies for the same ball. Some may decide to repeat the test several times and average the result, others may choose to discard the extreme results and take the middle result. In either case the children can see the need to repeat the experiment to get a more accurate outcome. To achieve even greater accuracy some children may wish to design and make a machine that drops the balls in exactly the same way every time.

Once the best bouncers have been found the children can try to explain their results. They should be able to suggest several factors such as weight, material, roughness of surface, presence of air and the tautness of the ball's surface. From this, they may be able to make simple generalizations: soft, squashy balls do not bounce well; heavy balls do not bounce well; smooth balls bounce better than rough balls. These generalizations could be tested with another set of balls. Older children should be able to appreciate that more than one factor can account for observed occurrences. The children may also be able to explain their findings. They may say heavy balls do not bounce well because they are being pulled down by the force of gravity more than light balls and that soft squashy and rough balls absorb more energy than smooth taut balls.

One experiment of this type may stimulate the children to suggest other investigations which different groups could carry out and report back to the rest of the class. They could test to see whether the ball bounced higher when it was dropped from a greater height and whether there was a steady increase in height of bounce with height of drop. Another group could test to find which surface, such as carpet squares, lino and trays of sand, were best to bounce balls on. They should find that a hard smooth surface is best as less energy is absorbed by the flooring material.

In order to see this springing movement the children should choose a ball that did not bounce well, such as a marble, and gently drop it on to a blown-up balloon. They should see that now the marble bounces well. The surface of the balloon changes shape as it is compressed and as the rubber springs back into place it pushes the marble away. The children can see that the best bouncers have this springiness either because the material is springy or because it acts like the balloon where the air is compressed and springs back into place.

COMPRESSED AIR TO CREATE SPRING

The children could investigate a collection of items that they can inflate, such as beach balls, swimming arm-bands and balloons, to discover what is needed to make them very springy. They should find out that there is no bounce without air, and the more air put into the object the more it will resist or spring back. They could test a football in the same way as before to find out how high it bounces with different amounts of air.

The compressed air in a balloon is a form of stored energy. When the air is released it can be used to create movement, as in 'jet-propelled' models using balloons (Chapter 4). The children can discuss how long this energy can be stored. Unless the container leaks or disintegrates the air can be stored indefinitely. Other mechanisms, such as pistons and pop-guns, also use compressed air to create movement.

A simple piston can be made with two new plastic syringes, without needles, connected with tubing (Figure 12.11). Pushing the end of one syringe compresses the air inside and forces out the end of the other syringe, showing that the energy put in one side of the tube is transmitted to the other.

Springs

The children can discover that although some materials like metal are not elastic, they can be made to act though they are by changing their shape, e.g. by winding wire around a pencil to make a spring. A collection of devices that use springs could be made which might include a jack-in-the-box, clothes pegs, hair grip, clockwork mechanisms, staplers, telephone flex, shock absorbers, spring balances and weighing machines.

Springs work in three ways, all of which can store energy. Some work by first being stretched and then springing back, such as the spring balance. Many others work by being compressed and then released. Bed and chair upholstery and toasters have this type of spring. The children can make a simple weighing machine that works by compression. Two containers are needed. One must be able to fit fairly closely inside the other (Figure 12.10). A scale is marked on the outside of the smaller container as weights are added.

The third set of springs work by being bent and they then try to spring back into a straighter form. If the children wind up a clock or clockwork toy they will see the coils become tighter, thus storing

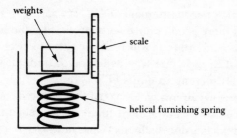

Figure 12.10 Making a simple weighing machine with a spring

the energy. Once the mechanism is released the spring unwinds to release movement energy to drive the rest of the machine. The children can time how long a toy car runs down after 1, 2, 3, etc. turns of the key.

Applying ideas of forces and energy in making moving models

Once the children have completed a topic that investigates aspects of forces and energy their grasp of the concepts can be reinforced and assessed by providing open-ended technology tasks that require them to apply their knowledge. For example:

- Design and make a machine that travels ½ metre and stops.
  The children could use twisted elastic to drive their device and work out how many twists are needed for the machine to travel ½ metre. Another group could make a cart that moves on a table that is pulled along by a falling weight (Figure 12.11).
- Make the fastest car you can that travels at least 3 metres.
  These children will need to carry out tests to assess different forms of propulsion, produce a streamlined shape and minimize friction of the working parts of the car but at the same time ensure that the wheels do not slip on the ground.
- Design and make a boat that can travel 1 metre.
  A paddling pool or large water trough used for water play can be used for tests. To produce propulsion the children might try a series of oars, sails, balloons for jet propulsion, paddles or propellers driven by elastic bands or electric motors. They need to test different materials and designs to produce streamlined

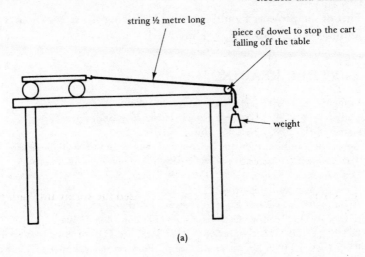

string ½ metre long

piece of dowel to stop the cart falling off the table

weight

(a)

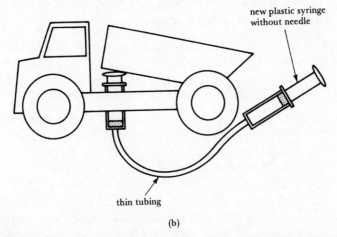

new plastic syringe without needle

thin tubing

(b)

Figure 12.11 (a) A cart that travels $\frac{1}{2}$ metre and stops (b) A tip-up truck using a 'piston'

stable boats. If they use sails they need to test different shapes and materials and think of a way to produce wind, perhaps from a balloon or flapping a magazine.

• Make a tip-up truck
  The children might use a balloon to push up the back of the truck or use a piston made from two syringes (Figure 12.11).

Part of the projects should include identifying the energy sources and forces and how they are involved.

FURTHER READING

Catherall, E. (1981) *Wind Power*. Hove: Wayland.

Catherall, E. (1982) *Levers and Ramps*. Hove: Wayland.

Catherall, E. (1983) *Elasticity*. Hove: Wayland.

Department of Education and Science and the Welsh Office (1989) *Science in the National Curriculum*. London: HMSO.

Department of Energy (1987) *Energy in Primary Science: Unit 1. Mechanical Energy*. London: Department of Energy.

Dixon, A. (1981) *Science Explorers: Bicycles*. London: A & C Black.

Dixon, A. (1982) *Science Explorers: Cranes*. London: A & C Black.

Fielding, D. (1984) *Looking at Science 5: A Closer Look*. Oxford: Basil Blackwell.

Fitzpatrick, J. (1986) *Science Spirals: Bounce, Stretch and Spring*. London: Hamish Hamilton.

Parker, S. (1985) *Step into Science: Mechanics*. London: Granada.

Radford, D. (1972) *Science from Toys: Stages 1 and 2 and Background*. London: Macdonald Educational/Schools Council.

C H A P T E R 13
Heating and Cooling

Ideally, during the early years, the children will have explored the effect of heating and cooling as they investigate the properties of different materials. Older children will need to learn to use a thermometer in order to study in more detail the changes that occur when familiar substances are heated and cooled. They should also measure and study temperature changes in the indoor and outside environment and how these temperatures can be controlled. This work is most appropriate for the oldest primary child as many of the investigations require accurate measurement and recording of temperature, patience to collect data over several days before a pattern emerges, and in a few cases negative numbers will be used. The majority of the older children will also be able to follow written instructions and to work independently, enabling groups to work at different times near a hot and cold water supply. Most activities can be carried out using hand-hot water. However, in some cases the teacher is advised to handle very hot water to help the children start an investigation safely.

The teacher is likely to initiate most of the investigations in this chapter. It is important therefore that the children predict the result of their activities before starting; observe carefully; look for patterns in the data collected; and try to explain for themselves what has happened. Hopefully when the children try the activities they will raise questions that require further investigation, which will involve them in designing and carrying out their own fair tests.

Measuring temperature

A few simple activities can be provided to demonstrate that our senses are insufficient to judge heat: vision is inadequate and the sense of touch unreliable. After discussing what visual clues might be used to judge whether something was hot or cold the teacher could challenge the children to sort a collection of pictures into hot or cold things. These might include pictures of ice-cream, ice lollies, snowmen, cans of orange, a refrigerator, a bonfire, hot-water bottles, mugs of tea, soup and a gas fire. Some of them need to be ambiguous; the tea may be iced or the hot-water bottle cold. The children should try to justify each decision as they sort the pictures. They may point out that some objects could not exist in a solid form unless they were very cold, such as the snowman and ice-cream or that the presence of flames indicates heat; however, they should come to the conclusion that the task is not possible in all cases unless they can feel the item.

The children are likely to be confident that they can accurately tell whether something is hot or cold by touch. They can then try a simple activity that demonstrates that this is not so. The children are provided with three bowls of water, one with cold water, one with very warm water and one with lukewarm water. Each child should put one hand in the very warm water and the other hand in the cold water at the same time. After about half a minute they should put both hands in the lukewarm water to discover that the hand from the very warm water now feels cold whereas the hand that had been in the cold water feels hot.

After an activity of this type the children are more likely to appreciate that a thermometer is needed to compare temperatures without being subjective. A large classroom thermometer is useful for large group or class activities. Many children do not realize that as the thermometer becomes hotter the column of alcohol lengthens. The children will need opportunities to discover this for themselves. They could be asked to think of ways of changing the level. They may suggest putting the thermometer on the radiator, putting it in ice, or holding it tightly in their hands. As the children try different things they can start to record the position of the alcohol as well as notice which way it moves. Initially the children might find it useful to colour in the position of the alcohol on a diagram that is the same size as the thermometer they are using.

A collection of different kinds of thermometers could prompt the children to realize that different designs are required in different situations. Some thermometers are dial-reading, some are read by using a scale, others are intended to be hung up, whereas others are for stirring or pushing into soil. Some are used for weather recordings, some for taking a sick person's temperature, and yet others are used for testing if a freezer is cold enough or if a joint of meat is cooked. Although the children might discuss mercury-filled thermometers that they may have at home to take their own temperatures these should *not* be used in school. The scales are difficult to read, and, if broken, the mercury gives off toxic vapour which can cause brain damage.

To help the children understand how a thermometer works they could make their own simple version. They need a small glass bottle between 10 cm and 20 cm tall and about one-third filled with coloured water. They also need narrow plastic tubing, which is put in the water but not touching the bottom of the bottle. Plasticine is used to hold the straw in place and to close the opening of the bottle. The plasticine should be pressed down firmly to seal the opening. If the bottle is then placed in a bowl of hot water the children should see the level of the coloured water rise noticeably. When it is put into cold water the level will drop (Figure 13.1a). Liquids usually expand when heated and contract when cooled, and this is the basis for most simple thermometers.

The experiment will be more successful if the tubing is thin, a glass bottle rather than plastic is used, and the bottle is only partially filled with water. If the bottle is completely filled with water the same effect will be seen but it takes longer for the movement of level to be seen and the level of water continues to rise for some time because the large amount of water takes time to reach a new uniform temperature. Manufactured thermometers contain small amounts of liquid so that the liquid can be uniformly heated quickly. If the bottle is partially filled with air the response is quicker because air expands more than water.

Other thermometers use the difference in expansion of metals to record temperature differences. Oven thermometers, usually found on the doors of cookers, use this principle. The children can see both how metal expands and how it can be used to record temperature by setting up the apparatus shown in Figure 13.1b.

The movement of the straw is slight so the children need to be warned to watch carefully. The children should then pour cold water over the copper tubing. The straw should not move.

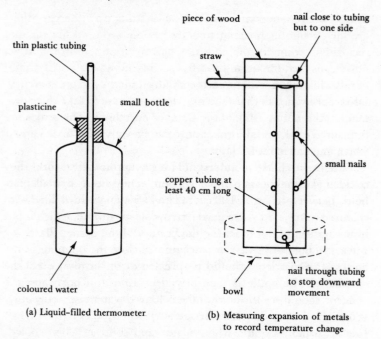

Figure 13.1 Thermometers

However, as hot water is poured over the tubing, the free end of the straw will rise slightly as the tubing expands upwards. When cold water is again poured over the tubing the straw will return to its original position. As the movement is small the children will probably need to repeat the action to be sure that the movement they have noticed is consistent. Whenever solid materials are used in long lengths builders have to take into account the effect of expansion and contraction in hot and cold weather. Small gaps are usually left between sections on bridges or between railway tracks. The children may also have noticed that electric wires outside are left to sag so that they will not break during cold spells in the winter when they contract.

When substances are heated they expand. Solids expand slightly and liquids expand considerably more, as the children will have found in heating metal and water to make thermometers. Gases expand a great deal. The children can see that air expands by putting a balloon over the neck of an empty glass bottle and placing the bottle in a bowl of hot water. The balloon will fill with expanded air. When the bottle is put into cold water the balloon will deflate. From this experiment the children may be able to explain why aerosol cans should not be heated.

Until children use thermometers they tend to have several misconceptions. They frequently assume that temperature is related to the nature of the object rather than to the temperature of the surrounding medium. Consequently they are puzzled that a thermometer will record a similar reading for all objects in a room even though some like metal feel colder than others. The children also often expect that temperature will be related to size or visible action. They expect that a large ice cube will be colder than a small one, no doubt because it takes longer to melt, whereas ice freezes at the same temperature whatever the size. In the same way they think that if the water is bubbling vigorously it must be hotter than when boiling with little motion visible. Children will only be able to adjust their views after many opportunities to take measurements for themselves not only in practical science investigations but during other activities such as cooking.

Temperatures of ourselves and the environment

Children can check for themselves that they are warm by feeling round the ribs, under the arms and inside the mouth. A thermometer will show them that they are warmer than the air around them, as the level of the liquid rises when they hold the bulb. They should not test under the tongue with a thermometer for reasons of safety. The children could feel other mammals, perhaps the class gerbil or a borrowed cat or dog, to confirm that they are also warm. They might discuss how penguins and seals keep warm in ice conditions. The teacher may wish to point out that this heat production by living things involves using up food.

The children could investigate whether adults or children find it easier to keep warm. In other words do large things cool at the same rate as small things? The children could use several plastic containers of different sizes with lids. A thermometer is placed through a hole in each lid. The containers can then be filled with hot water by the teacher and the change of temperature recorded every ten minutes. The children find this type of experiment much easier if they have a thermometer for each container. They can see the differences in temperature and do not make errors caused by reading the thermometer before it has adjusted to a new temperature. The children should find that small amounts of water lose heat more rapidly than large amounts. They may be able to relate this to the need to ensure babies are kept warm in winter.

Temperature differences in the school and immediate environment can be investigated. The children could take temperatures in a variety of places in the classroom; in a shady place outside; in an open space; on the surface of the playground; and on grass. They could also try different times of the day. The data collected could be recorded in graph form or as temperature maps. One of the important skills in science is to look for patterns in data and try to suggest what is causing the differences.

Once they have made a temperature map of the school they may be able to suggest why some places are hotter or cooler than others; perhaps the temperature was taken near a radiator, or in an area warmed by the sun, or near an open door. Modern schools often have computer controlled boilers which respond to changes of temperatures recorded in thermostats in different locations. In this case the children could discuss why it is important to locate these thermostats carefully. If they are located in naturally warm areas of the school the boilers will shut down before the cold areas are properly heated.

Discussions about the reasons for temperature differences outside the school are related to studies on different weather conditions. The children may consider at this point where a thermometer should be located to take meteorological recordings. On a sunny day the children will be able to feel the warmth from the direct rays of the sun. They could contrast this with the feeling of being in the shade and compare this with temperatures taken with a thermometer. The children might also compare the temperature very near the buildings and out in an open space. Temperatures are often affected by the warmth of the building so a location near the building would not give an accurate idea of the temperatures produced by the weather conditions. Similarly the children can see the effect of grass and concrete by taking temperatures on the surface of the playground; on the surface of the grass; and at a height away from the buildings. They should find that there is a difference in temperature as the concrete playground warms up quickly in the sun but loses its heat quickly when the sun has gone.

Different colours also affect temperature. To test this the children need two similar thermometers and coloured papers of the same type and size. The thermometers should be placed in the sunshine or under a table lamp so that the light falls equally on both. One thermometer is then covered with a sheet of black paper and the other with a sheet of white paper and they are left for about 15 to 30 minutes. The children should find that the black paper absorbs the sun's rays and becomes hotter. The children could then investigate different colours and compare rough and glossy paper.

When temperatures are taken for meteorological purposes it is important to eliminate other factors as much as possible. Consequently all official meteorological data are taken in similar conditions. Temperatures are recorded in a specially designed box, called a Stevenson's screen, that has slats all around to allow the air to circulate but ensures the thermometer is in the shade. The box is located away from buildings at a fixed height.

Ways of making heat

There are several ways of producing heat, such as processing food, friction, burning fuels, from electric currents and during some chemical reactions. The children will probably be able to itemize many of them. Most children will suggest burning things and they may also remember that they and other animals need food in order to keep warm and recall that when the bulb lights in an electric circuit it becomes hot.

Burning fuels is the major way of gaining heat in Britain and in some countries is the only method. With appropriate care the children can have practical experience with candles and a bonfire outside. For safety reasons the candles should be short and firmly stuck down in plasticine or sand. A variety of different coloured and shaped candles could be used. If they observe the candle carefully for about 10 minutes they could comment on the size, shape and colour of the flame. What colours can they see? Are the colours in the same place in each of the flames? What rises above the flames? What is the smell like? What makes the flame move? Does the colour of the wax alter the colour of the flames? Do fatter candles have bigger flames?

The children could have a small bonfire outside if an appropriate area is available. If they are involved in the planning and safety arrangements they are more likely to be careful with fire on other occasions. The plans may include deciding on: how to make a safe area for the fire with a ring of bricks; how to collect and store the dry material; what sort of day would be appropriate; and what safety precautions are needed. They should have a bucket of water and ensure everyone stands well back from the fire. The building, burning and extinguishing should be completed in one session and all the material burnt or subsequently removed so that it is not a temptation for an unsupervised repeat.

The teacher can help the children to observe details by questions such as: What do the flames look like? Do all the materials burn in the same way and at the same speed? What sounds, smells and colours do they notice? Does the wind have any effect? Observations might be recorded in a variety of forms, including poetry, pictures and tape recordings taken on the spot. The children will be able to see that the materials they have burnt have largely disappeared, so the teacher may wish to follow up their observations by explaining that all fuels, such as coal, wood, oil and natural gas, are used up as they are burnt, which has implications in conserving the earth's limited resources.

Heat is also created by friction. If the children rub their hands together they should feel the warmth produced. If they rub the side of a nail across sandpaper several times they should find the end of the nail becomes hot. The teacher could explain the idea of rubbing two surfaces together to make heat was the method of making fire used by early man. It is still used today to light matches, where the friction produced is enough to light the mixture of chemicals in the head. A flint in a gas lighter produces a small spark which ignites the gas.

To demonstrate that chemical reactions occasionally produce heat the children could put some plaster of Paris in a thin dish, add a little water and stir. After 10 minutes if they feel the bottom of the dish they should notice the heat produced.

Heat transfer

There are three ways in which heat can be transferred: radiation, conduction and convection.

RADIATION

Radiant heat has characteristics similar to light. It is given out by hot objects and travels in a straight line until it strikes another object. Radiant heat passes through air without warming it. This enables energy in the form of sunlight to reach us. Like light it is reflected by shiny surfaces and absorbed by dark matt surfaces, as the children will have discovered if they put thermometers under different coloured papers.

CONDUCTION

In conduction, heat energy moves through material. A metal rod becomes hot through conduction. Gas and liquids can also conduct heat. Heat flows by conduction from where there is a high temperature to where there is a low temperature. This continues until the temperatures equalize. Heat flows through different materials as long as they are touching.

CONVECTION

In convection a hot substance actually moves. It expands and therefore becomes less dense and tends to rise. Gas and liquids can be heated by convection but not solids.

Heating homes and schools

A graph or table could be compiled to show the ways the children's homes and the school are heated. The children could find the most popular method and ask their parents why they have chosen a particular system. Examples from catalogues could be sorted into method of heating and fuel type.

Most schools are heated by radiators. The caretaker might be prepared to explain how they and the heating system in the school works. If the radiators are turned on in the middle of the day the children can be asked to find out which part gets hot quickest. They should discover that the bottom becomes hottest first and as hot water rises the rest of the radiator becomes hot. The children can test the effect of mixing hot and cold water by using two similar bottles. One bottle is filled with warm coloured water and the other with cold water. A card is placed on top of the bottle with the cold water. It is then turned upside down and placed on top of the bottle with the warm water. The bottles should be kept directly in line with each other (Figure 13.2a). It helps to smear a bit of vaseline on the tops of the bottles to improve the contact. The children must try not to shake the bottles. When the card is carefully removed the children will be able to observe whether and how the two types of water mix. The experiment should be repeated with the bottles the

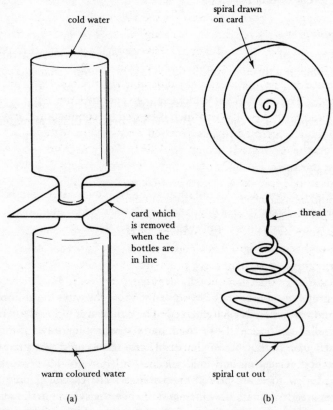

cold water

spiral drawn on card

card which is removed when the bottles are in line

thread

warm coloured water

spiral cut out

(a)   (b)

Figure 13.2   (a) Effects of mixing hot and cold water (b) Spiral cut-out

other way round. As water is heated it expands, so will not be as dense as the cold water. The less dense warm water will rise, by convection, into the cold water and mix. When the bottles are reversed they do not mix because the dense cold water will not rise.

The children may have noticed that papers left on top of the radiators tend to move slightly. Just as warm water moves upwards so does warm air. They could make mobiles to place over the radiator. A very simple one is to draw a spiral on to a card circle and cut it out to produce a spinning snake or patterned spiral mobile. A thread is attached to the centre to hang it up (Figure 13.2b). If the children keep it still, then blow increasingly hard on to it they should see that the rate of movement is influenced by moving air. Therefore when they see it turn above the radiator they know it is probably due to air rising. The speed it rotates depends upon how hot the radiator is. This experience helps children to appreciate that the air is moving within the classroom. As air is heated by the radiator it expands and rises. Cooler air takes its place. This type of movement is convection. Cool air is now in contact with the radiator which is heated by conduction. Once the cool air is warmed, the convection process is repeated.

As the room gets warmer, cold air is drawn in from outside. On the one hand a change of air in the room is essential; however, if this is too rapid the draughts become uncomfortable. The children could be asked to invent a draught detector. Small pieces of tissue paper fixed on a stick is one solution. The children can then test different parts of the classroom or school and locate the position of draughts on a plan. They could then think of ways to reduce the draughts and perhaps carry some of their ideas out. It is important that they realize that a totally draught-proof room may mean that there is no ventilation. To see how dangerous this would be the children could place a lighted candle underneath a glass jar. When the air is used up in the jar the flame goes out. Not only do animals need oxygen but so do flames. If the flame on a gas fire went out dangerous gases would escape and perhaps later cause an explosion. Firemen put oil or petrol fires out by pumping foam over them and stopping air getting to the flames. Water will not put out oil or petrol fires because the oil floats on the surface of the water.

Insulation and conduction

People maintain their body heat by wearing clothes. To prevent heat loss roofs and hot water tanks can be insulated in a similar way. The children can test different materials for lagging a water tank. They could use some bottles of the same size and cover all but one with different types of material, such as a range of cottons, wools, quilted materials, foil and plastic sheeting. One bottle should be left bare as a control. Once the bottles have been prepared the teacher should fill them with hot water. The most appropriate lagging material can be found by recording the temperature changes regularly. The children may extend the experiment by finding out whether it makes any difference if the material is wet. One way to design a fair experiment is to use two identical bottles and the same material and amount, with one of the materials soaked. It is more effective if the material is thick and wrapped several times around the bottles and very hot water is used in the bottles. The children should find the temperature drops quickly in the bottle with the soaked material and they may also see steam rising from this material. Evaporation of this water uses some of the heat. The teacher could relate this to explain why the children should wear appropriate clothes in the rain because once they get wet they will also become much colder.

Some house walls have cavity wall filling. The children could test different filling materials by using empty margarine boxes and coffee beakers. A beaker is placed in the middle of a box and the space round the beaker is filled with different materials. The children might use torn up paper, polystyrene, scraps of fabric and cotton-wool. One box should be left empty as the control. The beakers are filled with hot water and the loss of temperature recorded regularly. Once the best material is found the children could test to see whether a lid, or roof, makes any difference to the heat retention.

Heat energy passes along solid materials by conduction. Good insulators are poor conductors. The children can try to sort different materials into insulators and conductors. One simple way is to use a hot-water bottle full of hot water. Different plates, such as paper, glass, foil, china, plastic and tin, are put on it and the children feel which plates become warm quickly. A variety of spoons can also be tested by placing them in hot water. If the children feel the handles after 5 or 10 minutes they should find that the metal spoons have become hot but the others have not. Metals are in general good conductors whereas glass, wood, plastic and fabric are poor conductors.

The children can discuss the relative value of each type of spoon. Plastic and wooden spoons are safe to hold when stirring hot things but wooden spoons are not easy to manufacture in a variety of different shapes and plastic melts if it gets too hot. Consequently many spoons for use in the kitchen are metal with plastic handles. The children could collect pictures of kitchen utensils and equipment and mark which are safe to handle and those that need to be handled using another insulator such as an oven glove. A collection of tea pots, made of different materials, could be made and tested to discover which shape and material retains heat longest. Once a poorly insulated tea pot has been found the children could design and test tea-cosies for it.

The movement of heat through metal could be investigated further. The children could be asked to find out whether only heat moves along metal. The children may be able to suggest how they could solve the problem. One method is to use three beakers. One should be filled with hot water and the other with ice cubes. One metal spoon is placed in the hot water and one is placed in the ice cubes. A third needs be left in an empty beaker as the control. The children should be able to feel the difference after 5 to 10 minutes. The movement of heat through metal can also be demonstrated by setting up equipment as shown in Figure 13.3. As the heat travels along the metal the wax melts and drops off. The children could fix the wax in different places along the metal to see how far the heat travels before being ineffective.

Changing materials by heating or cooling

Matter can be changed from one state to another by adding or removing heat energy. The children will be able to think of many examples from their own experience: boiling kettles, wax and chocolate melting, ponds freezing and steam condensing. Some of these changes can be explored in more detail.

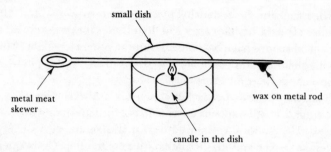

Figure 13.3 Movement of heat through metal

Experiments using water not only help children to understand the connection between liquids, solids and gases but also provide a good foundation leading to understanding of the water cycle. The children may have already investigated how ice is formed in their early years (Chapter 2). This work needs to be recapped and extended.

On a very cold day the children could look for places where water has frozen. If they look carefully at puddles they may notice that shallow puddles have completely frozen but deep ones or ponds may only have frozen around the edge or on the surface. This observation is important from a safety point of view to enable the children to appreciate how dangerous it is to play on the surface of frozen ponds where the ice is likely to be thin in the middle. If the children tread on the puddles they might also notice how the ice breaks. Again questions will help the children to think about their observations. Are the edges sharp, straight or curved? Are the pieces of ice the same thickness? What happens to the ice when it is handled? What does melting ice feel like? The children may also be able to see icicles and might be able to suggest why they have occurred in one place but not another and how they develop. Icicles will form in sheltered places where there is a slow flow of water. The children might relate their observations to the formation of stalactites.

The teacher could ask children to think about their experiences with ice and predict whether ice will always float. They might recall ice floating in drinks and the ice formed on the surface of the puddles but they may be uncertain whether it will float in all situations. The children could make different shaped pieces of ice and freeze them. Before testing them to see if they float they should predict not only whether they will float but how. For example, will a long narrow shape float upright completely under the water? They will find that all ice floats with the bulk of it below the surface. This is important for shipping as icebergs with hidden ice below the surface of the sea constitute a considerable danger.

To further explore the properties of ice the children can be given glass bottles with corks. If the bottles are filled to the top with water, the corks fitted firmly on the top and put outside on a freezing night ice will form in them. However, as ice takes up more space than water the ice will force the corks out of the bottles on columns of ice. The glass bottles should be each left in a bucket because occasionally the bottle cracks with the force of expanding ice. This is a dramatic way to demonstrate how ice is an important factor in weathering and breaking down rocks. Water seeps into cracks, freezes and forces the crack further apart. This action repeated several times breaks the rock or road surface up. Once the children understand that the same amount of ice takes up more space than the equivalent water they may be able to understand why ice floats. The amount of matter is the same in both cases but the molecular structure in the case of ice is more spread out in the greater volume. This makes the ice less dense than water. The less dense ice floats on the more dense water.

Ice balloons are an exciting way to explore the properties of ice. Balloons are filled with water, the ends tied and put into a freezer. They should be put inside plastic carrier bags in case they burst. After about three days groups of children can tear away the rubber, and observe and investigate the results. They might look at the shape and types of ice produced, how it feels, whether it melts in the same way in water and air, or what happens when salt, sugar or paint is added. The children may wish to make ice balloons in different ways. They may try to make a multi-coloured balloon by adding different coloured water at different times in the freezing process, or try different solutions such as salt and water or coffee and water. The children should find that a strong salt solution does not freeze in an ordinary household freezer. This is because the salt solution has a lower freezing point than pure water.

They could try an experiment to investigate the effect of mixing salt and ice further. The children need two jars of the same size.

The jars are filled with crushed ice. The ice can be broken up by putting it into a thick plastic bag and hitting it gently with a hammer. A heaped spoonful of salt is then stirred into one jar and the temperature of each jar measured and recorded every 5 minutes over a period of 20 minutes. The children should discover that the ice on its own will stay at a temperature of about 0°C. The mixed ice and salt will produce a temperature below 0°C and will melt more quickly. In theory a liquid freezes at the same temperature as it melts. The freezing point of the salt mixture is lower than the pure water, as the children will have found with the ice balloons made of salt solution. Temperatures in Britain are very unlikely to drop low enough to freeze a salt solution, which is why salt is put on icy or snowy roads. The children can investigate whether other substances such as sand or sugar have the same effect.

When water is heated to boiling point it changes into steam, i.e. a gas. If the children watch a saucepan with a lid or a kettle with a whistle being boiled they should notice the steam coming off is strong enough to make a whistle or lift the lid. The use of steam as a power source in steam engines could then be discussed. When the kettle is boiling, if the teacher places a cold plate in the path of the steam the children will see the water condense. The children can then look for examples where condensation has occurred and try to explain them, i.e. where warm air meets a cold surface.

The children might like to taste cooled boiled water and compare its taste to ordinary water. They may notice that it tastes flat because the air has been boiled out. However this is not a irreversible change because if the boiled water is put into a container, half full, and shaken vigorously the flat taste will go.

There are many situations where hot things cool or cold things warm up when there has been no apparent addition or removal of heat. The teacher could ask the children why a cup of tea cools or ice melts in the classroom. Unless a force or energy is applied things will change their temperature until they reach the temperature of the surroundings. The rate this occurs depends on different factors. The children can be prompted to think of some of these factors by being asked to suggest ways of cooling hot tea. They may suggest putting it somewhere cold, blowing on it, putting it in a poorly insulated container or pouring it into a saucer. They can then test some of these ideas. If they wanted to test how an open saucer might cool quicker than a mug they could put the same amount of hot water into three or four containers that will give different surface areas and record the temperature changes.

Similar factors are important in the rate of evaporation. The children could list the factors they think are important, such as kind of water, surrounding temperature, wind conditions, amount of water, size or shape of container. Different groups of children could design and set up a fair investigation to test each and then report back to the whole class. In each investigation only the variable they are testing should change. They could also test to see if other liquids evaporate in the same way as water. They could observe what happens to small drops of different liquids such as milk, oil, or washing-up liquid compared with drops of water.

Cooking is a good way to enable children to see the effect of heating and cooling substances other than water. Some of these changes are reversible but others are not. When milk is boiled the change is irreversible because some of the enzymes have been broken down. The children will see that the milk looks and tastes different after boiling. They could also observe the effect of heating and cooling butter, margarine, cheese and chocolate either as part of cooking activities or by putting different substances in small containers and floating them on top of hot water in a bowl and then on cold water to observe changes caused by changes of heat.

Art also provides many opportunities to encourage scientific observations and to raise questions. For example, if wax is used for batik the children will be able to see the effect of melting and cooling wax, and pottery can involve observing the effect of firing clays and glazes. If the teachers have an awareness of the knowledge and skills required for the primary child they will be able to maximize these opportunities to help the children both to further their scientific understanding and to see how it can be applied.

FURTHER READING

Brown, C., Brown, C., Edwards, E., Roberts, A. and Young, B. (1985) *Exploring Changes*. Cambridge: Cambridge University Press.

Department of Education and Science and the Welsh Office (1989) *Science in the National Curriculum*. London: HMSO.

Children and Primary Science

Department of Energy *Energy in Primary Science: Heat*. London: Department of Energy.

Driver, R., Guesne, E. and Tiberghien, A. (eds) (1985) *Children's Ideas in Science*. Milton Keynes: Open University Press.

Gilbert, C. and Matthews, P. (1981–5) *Look! Primary Science Project*. Edinburgh: Oliver and Boyd.

Hargraves, E. and Brooks, J. (1986) *Science through Infant Topics: Teachers' Books A-C*. Harlow: Longman.

Hobbs, D., Hudson, J., Moreland, A. and Slack, D. (1985) *Science Horizons Level 2a: Keeping Our Home Warm*. London: Macmillan Education.

Jennings, J. (1982) *The Young Scientist Investigates: Heat*. Oxford: Oxford University Press.

Murray, E. and Crittenden, R. (1986) *Science Scene Setters: Heat*. British Gas Corporation.

Index

Index

Index

Living

There are powerful assumptions about gender divisions inscribed in the built environment. Housing is the site of some complex processes in society. Within it, future generations of workers are reared, the sexual division of domestic labour is enacted, class-status divisions are affirmed. In making and remaking their homes, women and men define their place in the world and are defined by it. These processes have physical manifestations which are subject to central and local government intervention. Key points are the relationship of housing form to the renewal of the workforce; the location of housing in relation to women's and men's employment; design standards within the home; the imagery of housing as intended by architects and the people who live in it.

Taking an historical perspective, this book is the first to make a complete examination of the relationship of gender to housing design. Design is seen in broad terms, and revealed as part of the social process of society, rather than a separate sphere in which the architect has sole responsibility for decision making. Many of the ills of the contemporary environment can be traced to the barriers that have been built up between the concerns of social policy, planning and architecture. By breaking down these barriers through a synoptic study of how gender assumptions have operated in the design of housing, this book points the way to how improvements in design and in the built environment may be better achieved.